MW00845125

Learning Python Design Patterns

Second Edition

Leverage the power of Python design patterns to solve real-world problems in software architecture and design

Chetan Giridhar

BIRMINGHAM - MUMBAI

Learning Python Design Patterns

Second Edition

Copyright © 2016 Packt Publishing

All rights reserved. No part of this book may be reproduced, stored in a retrieval system, or transmitted in any form or by any means, without the prior written permission of the publisher, except in the case of brief quotations embedded in critical articles or reviews.

Every effort has been made in the preparation of this book to ensure the accuracy of the information presented. However, the information contained in this book is sold without warranty, either express or implied. Neither the author, nor Packt Publishing, and its dealers and distributors will be held liable for any damages caused or alleged to be caused directly or indirectly by this book.

Packt Publishing has endeavored to provide trademark information about all of the companies and products mentioned in this book by the appropriate use of capitals. However, Packt Publishing cannot guarantee the accuracy of this information.

First published: November 2013

Second edition: February 2016

Production reference: 1080216

Published by Packt Publishing Ltd.
Livery Place
35 Livery Street
Birmingham B3 2PB, UK.

ISBN 978-1-78588-803-8

www.packtpub.com

Credits

Author
Chetan Giridhar

Reviewer
Maurice HT Ling

Commissioning Editor
Kunal Parikh

Acquisition Editor
Denim Pinto

Content Development Editor
Merint Thomas Mathew

Technical Editor
Chinmay S. Puranik

Copy Editor
Tasneem Fatehi

Project Coordinator
Suzanne Coutinho

Proofreader
Safis Editing

Indexer
Priya Sane

Graphics
Kirk D'Penha

Production Coordinator
Shantanu N. Zagade

Cover Work
Shantanu N. Zagade

Foreword

"Controlling complexity is the essence of computer programming."

– Brian Kernighan

"All problems in computer science can be solved by another level of indirection (abstraction)."

– David Wheeler

The preceding two quotes by two well known computer scientists illustrate the problem faced by the modern software designer—coming up with a good, stable, reusable, flexible solution to a software design problem.

Design patterns solve the preceding problems in the most elegant way. Design patterns abstract and present in neat, well-defined components and interfaces the experience of many software designers and architects over many years of solving similar problems. These are solutions that have withstood the test of time with respect to reusability, flexibility, scalability, and maintainability.

There have been many books on design patterns with the well-known Gang of Four (GoF) book forming the cornerstone of nearly the entire domain.

However, in this era of web and mobile computing, where programs tend to get written in high-level languages such as Python, Ruby, and Clojure, there is often a need for books that translate the rather esoteric language used in such books into more familiar terms, with reusable code written in these newer, more dynamic programming languages. This is especially true when it comes to newbie programmers who often tend to get lost in the complexities of design versus implementation and often require an expert helping hand.

This book fulfills that role very well. It uses the template of design patterns as laid out in the GoF book and adds a few others as well for completion — but before jumping into the patterns itself, gives the young and inexperienced reader the fundamentals of software design principles that have gone into the thinking behind the creation and evolution of these design patterns. It doesn't walk the gentle reader blindly into the maze of the pattern world, but lays out the fundamentals well before opening that door and carrying the reader along that path of learning.

The book is written with Python as the language for implementing the sample code for the patterns — and this makes excellent sense. As someone who has spent more than 12 years in the company of this wonderful programming language, I can attest to its beauty and simplicity and its effectiveness in solving problems ranging from routine to the most complex. Python is ideally suited to the rookie and young programmer, and with the ease of learning it, it is also a lot of fun to code in. The young programmer would find their time spent in the company of Python along in this book very rewarding and fruitful.

Chetan Giridhar has been working and contributing to Python for well over 7 years. He is ideally suited for the job of penning a book like this, as he has gone through some of the cycles of learning the complexities of implementation and design himself and has learned well through that process. He is a well-known speaker on a number of varied topics in Python and has delivered well-attended talks at Python conferences, such as PyCon India. He was amongst the invited speakers for conferences in the USA, Asia-Pacific, and New Zealand.

I believe this book, *Learning Python Design Patterns, Second Edition*, would be an excellent addition to the *Learning* series by Packt Publishing and would provide a set of skills to the toolbox of the young Python programmer that would take them gently and expertly to being able to design modular and efficient programs in Python.

Anand B Pillai
CTO — Skoov.com
Board Member — Python Software Foundation
Founder — Bangalore Python User's Group

About the Author

Chetan Giridhar is a technology leader, open source enthusiast, and Python developer. He has written multiple articles on technology and development practices in magazines such as LinuxForYou and Agile Record, and has published technical papers in the Python Papers journal. He has been a speaker at PyCon conferences such as PyCon India, Asia-Pacific, and New Zealand and loves working on real-time communications, distributed systems, and cloud applications. Chetan has been a reviewer at Packt Publishing and has contributed to books on IPython Visualizations and Core Python.

I'd like to thank the Packt Publishing team, especially Merint Thomas Mathew, and the technical reviewer, Maurice HT Ling, for bringing out the best content in this book. Special thanks to my mentor, Anand B Pillai, for graciously accepting to review this book and writing the foreword. This book wouldn't be possible without the blessings of my parents, Jyotsana and Jayant Giridhar, and constant support and encouragement from my wife, Deepti, and my daughter, Pihu!

About the Reviewer

Maurice HT Ling has been programming in Python since 2003. Having completed his Ph D in bioinformatics and B Sc (honors) in molecular and cell biology from The University of Melbourne, he is currently a research fellow in Nanyang Technological University, Singapore, and an honorary fellow at The University of Melbourne, Australia. Maurice is the chief editor for computational and mathematical biology, and co-editor for The Python Papers. Recently, Maurice cofounded the first synthetic biology startup in Singapore, AdvanceSyn Pte. Ltd., as a director and chief technology officer. He is also the principal partner of Colossus Technologies LLP, Singapore. His research interests lie in life—biological life, artificial life, and artificial intelligence—using computer science and statistics as tools to understand life and its numerous aspects. In his free time, Maurice likes to read, enjoy a cup of coffee, write his personal journal, or philosophize on various aspects of life. You can reach him at his website and on his LinkedIn profile at `http://maurice.vodien.com` and `http://www.linkedin.com/in/mauriceling`, respectively.

www.PacktPub.com

Support files, eBooks, discount offers, and more

For support files and downloads related to your book, please visit www.PacktPub.com.

Did you know that Packt offers eBook versions of every book published, with PDF and ePub files available? You can upgrade to the eBook version at www.PacktPub.com and as a print book customer, you are entitled to a discount on the eBook copy. Get in touch with us at service@packtpub.com for more details.

At www.PacktPub.com, you can also read a collection of free technical articles, sign up for a range of free newsletters and receive exclusive discounts and offers on Packt books and eBooks.

https://www2.packtpub.com/books/subscription/packtlib

Do you need instant solutions to your IT questions? PacktLib is Packt's online digital book library. Here, you can search, access, and read Packt's entire library of books.

Why subscribe?

- Fully searchable across every book published by Packt
- Copy and paste, print, and bookmark content
- On demand and accessible via a web browser

Free access for Packt account holders

If you have an account with Packt at www.PacktPub.com, you can use this to access PacktLib today and view 9 entirely free books. Simply use your login credentials for immediate access.

Table of Contents

Preface   **vii**

Chapter 1: Introduction to Design Patterns   **1**

Understanding object-oriented programming   **2**
Objects   2
Classes   2
Methods   3
Major aspects of object-oriented programming   **3**
Encapsulation   3
Polymorphism   4
Inheritance   4
Abstraction   5
Composition   6
Object-oriented design principles   **6**
The open/close principle   6
The inversion of control principle   7
The interface segregation principle   7
The single responsibility principle   8
The substitution principle   8
The concept of design patterns   **8**
Advantages of design patterns   10
Taxonomy of design patterns   10
Context – the applicability of design patterns   10

Patterns for dynamic languages	**11**
Classifying patterns	**11**
Creational patterns	11
Structural patterns	12
Behavioral patterns	12
Summary	**12**
Chapter 2: The Singleton Design Pattern	**13**
Understanding the Singleton design pattern	**14**
Implementing a classical Singleton in Python	14
Lazy instantiation in the Singleton pattern	**15**
Module-level Singletons	**16**
The Monostate Singleton pattern	**16**
Singletons and metaclasses	**18**
A real-world scenario – the Singleton pattern, part 1	**19**
A real-world scenario – the Singleton pattern, part 2	**21**
Drawbacks of the Singleton pattern	**23**
Summary	**24**
Chapter 3: The Factory Pattern – Building Factories to Create Objects	**25**
Understanding the Factory pattern	**25**
The Simple Factory pattern	**26**
The Factory Method pattern	**28**
Implementing the Factory Method	29
Advantages of the Factory method pattern	32
The Abstract Factory pattern	**32**
Implementing the Abstract Factory pattern	34
The Factory method versus Abstract Factory method	**36**
Summary	**37**
Chapter 4: The Façade Pattern – Being Adaptive with Façade	**39**
Understanding Structural design patterns	**40**
Understanding the Façade design pattern	**40**
A UML class diagram	**41**
Façade	42
System	42
Client	43
Implementing the Façade pattern in the real world	**43**
The principle of least knowledge	**47**
Frequently asked questions	**47**
Summary	**48**

Chapter 5: The Proxy Pattern – Controlling Object Access   49

Understanding the Proxy design pattern   50
A UML class diagram for the Proxy pattern   52
Understanding different types of Proxies   53
     A virtual proxy   53
     A remote proxy   53
     A protective proxy   54
     A smart proxy   54
The Proxy pattern in the real world   54
Advantages of the Proxy pattern   58
Comparing the Façade and Proxy patterns   58
Frequently asked questions   58
Summary   59

Chapter 6: The Observer Pattern – Keeping Objects in the Know   61

Introducing Behavioral patterns   62
Understanding the Observer design pattern   62
     A UML class diagram for the Observer pattern   64
The Observer pattern in the real world   65
The Observer pattern methods   69
     The pull model   69
     The push model   70
Loose coupling and the Observer pattern   70
The Observer pattern – advantages and disadvantages   71
Frequently asked questions   71
Summary   72

Chapter 7: The Command Pattern – Encapsulating Invocation   73

Introducing the Command pattern   74
Understanding the Command design pattern   74
     A UML class diagram for the Command pattern   76
Implementing the Command pattern in the real world   79
     Design considerations   79
Advantages and disadvantages of Command patterns   83
Frequently asked questions   83
Summary   84

Chapter 8: The Template Method Pattern – Encapsulating Algorithm — 85

Defining the Template Method pattern — 86
Understanding the Template Method design pattern — 88
A UML class diagram for the Template Method pattern — 90
The Template Method pattern in the real world — 92
The Template Method pattern – hooks — 96
The Hollywood principle and the Template Method — 97
The advantages and disadvantages of the Template Method pattern — 97
Frequently asked questions — 98
Summary — 98

Chapter 9: Model-View-Controller – Compound Patterns — 99

An introduction to Compound patterns — 100
The Model-View-Controller pattern — 100
Model – knowledge of the application — 102
View – the appearance — 103
Controller – the glue — 103
A UML class diagram for the MVC design pattern — 105
The MVC pattern in the real world — 107
Modules — 107
Benefits of the MVC pattern — 114
Frequently asked questions — 115
Summary — 115

Chapter 10: The State Design Pattern — 117

Defining the State design pattern — 117
Understanding the State design pattern — 118
Understanding the State design pattern with a UML diagram — 120
A simple example of the State design pattern — 120
The State design pattern with v3.5 implementation — 122
Advantages/disadvantages of the State pattern — 125
Summary — 126

Chapter 11: AntiPatterns	**127**
An introduction to AntiPatterns	**128**
Software development AntiPatterns	**129**
Spaghetti code	129
Golden Hammer	130
Lava Flow	131
Copy-and-paste or cut-and-paste programming	131
Software architecture AntiPatterns	**132**
Reinventing the wheel	132
Vendor lock-in	133
Design by committee	133
Summary	**134**
Index	**135**

Preface

Design patterns are among the most powerful methods of building large software systems. With an increasing focus on optimized software architecture and design, it is important that software architects think about optimizations in object creation, code structure, and interaction between objects at the architecture or design level. This makes sure that the cost of software maintenance is low, and code can be easily reused and is adaptable to change. Moreover, providing frameworks for reusability and separation of concerns is key to software development today.

What this book covers

Chapter 1, *Introduction to Design Patterns*, goes through the basics of object-oriented programming and discusses object-oriented design principles in detail. This chapter gives a brief introduction to the concept of design patterns so that you will be able to appreciate the context and application of design patterns in software development.

Chapter 2, *The Singleton Design Pattern*, covers one of the simplest and well-known Creational design patterns used in application development—the Singleton design pattern. The different ways in which we can create a Singleton pattern in Python are also covered in this chapter along with examples. This chapter also covers the Monostate (or Borg) design pattern, which is a variant of the Singleton design pattern.

Chapter 3, *The Factory Pattern – Building Factories to Create Objects*, discusses another creational pattern, the Factory pattern. You will also learn about the Factory Method pattern and Abstract Factory pattern with a UML diagram, real-world scenarios, and Python v3.5 implementations.

Chapter 4, The Façade Pattern – Being Adaptive with Façade, shows you another type of design pattern, the Structural design pattern. We will be introduced to the concept of Façade and learn how it is applicable to software design with the help of the Façade design pattern. You'll also learn its implementation with a sample Python application using a real-world scenario.

Chapter 5, The Proxy Pattern – Controlling Object Access, deals with the Proxy pattern that falls into the category of Structural design patterns. We will be introduced to the Proxy as a concept and discuss the design pattern and see how it is used in software application development. You'll also learn about the different variants of the Proxy pattern—Virtual Proxy, Smart Proxy, Remote Proxy, and Protective Proxy.

Chapter 6, The Observer Pattern – Keeping Objects in the Know, talks about the third type of design pattern—the behavioral design pattern. We will be introduced to the Observer design pattern with examples. In this chapter, you'll learn how to implement the Push and Pull models of the Observer pattern and the principles of loose coupling. We'll also see how this pattern is critical when it comes to applying it to cloud applications and distributed systems.

Chapter 7, The Command Pattern – Encapsulating Invocation, tells you about the Command design pattern. We will be introduced to the Command design pattern and discuss how it is used in software application development with a real-world scenario and Python implementation. We will also study two main aspects of the Command pattern—an implementation of redo/rollback operations and asynchronous task execution.

Chapter 8, The Template Method Pattern – Encapsulating Algorithm, discusses the Template design pattern. Like the Command pattern, the Template pattern falls into the category of Behavioral patterns. Here, we discuss the Template method pattern, and you will learn about Hooks with an implementation. We'll also cover the Hollywood principle that helps us appreciate this pattern better.

Chapter 9, Model-View-Controller – Compound Patterns, talks about Compound patterns. We will be introduced to the Model-View-Controller design pattern and discuss how it is used in software application development. MVC is easily one of the most used design patterns; in fact, many Python frameworks are based on this principle. You will learn about the details of MVC implementation with an example application written in Python Tornado (a framework used by Facebook).

Chapter 10, The State Design Pattern, introduces you to the State design pattern, which falls into the category of Behavioral patterns just like the Command or Template design patterns. We will discuss how it is used in software application development.

Chapter 11, AntiPatterns, tells you about AntiPatterns—what we shouldn't do as architects or software engineers.

What you need for this book

All you need is Python v3.5, and you can download it from
https://www.python.org/downloads/.

Who this book is for

This book is for Python developers and software architects who care about software
design principles and details of application development aspects in Python. It
requires a basic understanding of programming concepts and beginner-level Python
development experience. It will also be helpful for students and teachers in live
learning environments.

Conventions

In this book, you will find a number of text styles that distinguish between different
kinds of information. Here are some examples of these styles and an explanation of
their meaning.

Code words in text, database table names, folder names, filenames, file extensions,
pathnames, dummy URLs, user input, and Twitter handles are shown as follows:
"The Car object will have attributes such as fuel level, isSedan, speed, and
steering wheel and coordinates."

A block of code is set as follows:

```
class Person(object):
    def __init__(self, name, age):  #constructor
        self.name = name     #data members/ attributes
        self.age = age
    def get_person(self,):   # member function
        return "<Person (%s, %s)>" % (self.name, self.age)


p = Person("John", 32)     # p is an object of type Person
print("Type of Object:", type(p), "Memory Address:", id(p))
```

New terms and **important words** are shown in bold. Words that you see on the screen, for example, in menus or dialog boxes, appear in the text like this: "In Python, the concept of encapsulation (data and method hiding) is not implicit, as it doesn't have keywords such as **public**, **private**, and **protected** (in languages such as C++ or Java) that are required to support encapsulation."

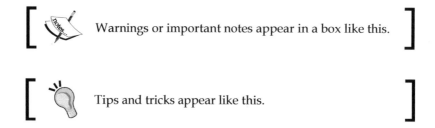

Warnings or important notes appear in a box like this.

Tips and tricks appear like this.

Reader feedback

Feedback from our readers is always welcome. Let us know what you think about this book—what you liked or disliked. Reader feedback is important for us as it helps us develop titles that you will really get the most out of.

To send us general feedback, simply e-mail feedback@packtpub.com, and mention the book's title in the subject of your message.

If there is a topic that you have expertise in and you are interested in either writing or contributing to a book, see our author guide at www.packtpub.com/authors.

Customer support

Now that you are the proud owner of a Packt book, we have a number of things to help you to get the most from your purchase.

Downloading the example code

You can download the example code files from your account at http://www.packtpub.com for all the Packt Publishing books you have purchased. If you purchased this book elsewhere, you can visit http://www.packtpub.com/support and register to have the files e-mailed directly to you.

Errata

Although we have taken every care to ensure the accuracy of our content, mistakes do happen. If you find a mistake in one of our books—maybe a mistake in the text or the code—we would be grateful if you could report this to us. By doing so, you can save other readers from frustration and help us improve subsequent versions of this book. If you find any errata, please report them by visiting http://www.packtpub.com/submit-errata, selecting your book, clicking on the **Errata Submission Form** link, and entering the details of your errata. Once your errata are verified, your submission will be accepted and the errata will be uploaded to our website or added to any list of existing errata under the Errata section of that title.

To view the previously submitted errata, go to https://www.packtpub.com/books/content/support and enter the name of the book in the search field. The required information will appear under the **Errata** section.

Piracy

Piracy of copyrighted material on the Internet is an ongoing problem across all media. At Packt, we take the protection of our copyright and licenses very seriously. If you come across any illegal copies of our works in any form on the Internet, please provide us with the location address or website name immediately so that we can pursue a remedy.

Please contact us at copyright@packtpub.com with a link to the suspected pirated material.

We appreciate your help in protecting our authors and our ability to bring you valuable content.

Questions

If you have a problem with any aspect of this book, you can contact us at questions@packtpub.com, and we will do our best to address the problem.

1
Introduction to Design Patterns

In this chapter, we will go through the basics of object-oriented programming and discuss the object-oriented design principles in detail. This will get us prepared for the advanced topics covered later in the book. This chapter will also give a brief introduction to the concept of design patterns so that you will be able to appreciate the context and application of design patterns in software development. Here we also classify the design patterns under three main aspects—creational, structural, and Behavioral patterns. So, essentially, we will cover the following topics in this chapter:

- Understanding object-oriented programming
- Discussing object-oriented design principles
- Understanding the concept of design patterns and their taxonomy and context
- Discussing patterns for dynamic languages
- Classifying patterns—creational pattern, structural pattern, and behavioral pattern

Understanding object-oriented programming

Before you start learning about design patterns, it's always good to cover the basics and go through object-oriented paradigms in Python. The object-oriented world presents the concept of *objects* that have attributes (data members) and procedures (member functions). These functions are responsible for manipulating the attributes. For instance, take an example of the `Car` object. The `Car` object will have attributes such as `fuel level`, `isSedan`, `speed`, and `steering wheel` and `coordinates`, and the methods would be `accelerate()` to increase the speed and `takeLeft()` to make the car turn left. Python has been an object-oriented language since it was first released. As they say, *everything in Python is an object*. Each class instance or variable has its own memory address or identity. Objects, which are instances of classes, interact among each other to serve the purpose of an application under development. Understanding the core concepts of object-oriented programming involves understanding the concepts of objects, classes, and methods.

Objects

The following points describe objects:

- They represent entities in your application under development.
- Entities interact among themselves to solve real-world problems.
- For example, Person is an entity and Car is an entity. Person drives Car to move from one location to the other.

Classes

Classes help developers to represent real-world entities:

- Classes define objects in attributes and behaviors. Attributes are data members and behaviors are manifested by the member functions
- Classes consist of constructors that provide the initial state for these objects
- Classes are like templates and hence can be easily reused

For example, class `Person` will have attributes `name` and `age` and member function `gotoOffice()` that defines his behavior for travelling to office for work.

Methods

The following points talk about what methods do in the object-oriented world:

- They represent the behavior of the object
- Methods work on attributes and also implement the desired functionality

A good example of a class and object created in Python v3.5 is given here:

```
class Person(object):
    def __init__(self, name, age):  #constructor
        self.name = name    #data members/ attributes
        self.age = age
    def get_person(self,):   # member function
        return "<Person (%s, %s)>" % (self.name, self.age)


p = Person("John", 32)    # p is an object of type Person
print("Type of Object:", type(p), "Memory Address:", id(p))
```

The output of the preceding code should look as follows:

```
Type of Object: <class '__main__.Person'> Memory Address: 4329015224
```

Major aspects of object-oriented programming

Now that we have understood the basics of object-oriented programming, let's dive into the major aspects of OOP.

Encapsulation

The key features of encapsulation are as follows:

- An object's behavior is kept hidden from the outside world or objects keep their state information private.
- Clients can't change the object's internal state by directly acting on them; rather, clients request the object by sending messages. Based on the type of requests, objects may respond by changing their internal state using special member functions such as get and set.

- In Python, the concept of encapsulation (data and method hiding) is not implicit, as it doesn't have keywords such as **public**, **private**, and **protected** (in languages such as C++ or Java) that are required to support encapsulation. Of course, accessibility can be made private by prefixing __ in the variable or function name.

Polymorphism

The major features of polymorphism are as follows:

- Polymorphism can be of two types:
    - An object provides different implementations of the method based on input parameters
    - The same interface can be used by objects of different types

- In Python, polymorphism is a feature built-in for the language. For example, the + operator can act on two integers to add them or can work with strings to concatenate them

In the following example, strings, tuples, or lists can all be accessed with an integer index. This shows how Python demonstrates polymorphism in built-in types:

```
a = "John"
b = (1,2,3)
c = [3,4,6,8,9]
print(a[1], b[0], c[2])
```

Inheritance

The following points help us understand the inheritance process better:

- Inheritance indicates that one class derives (most of its) functionality from the parent class.

- Inheritance is described as an option to reuse functionality defined in the base class and allow independent extensions of the original software implementation.

- Inheritance creates hierarchy via the relationships among objects of different classes. Python, unlike Java, supports multiple inheritance (inheriting from multiple base classes).

In the following code example, `class A` is the base class and `class B` derives its features from `class A`. So, the methods of `class A` can be accessed by the object of `class B`:

```
class A:
    def a1(self):
        print("a1")

class B(A):
    def b(self):
        print("b")



b = B()
b.a1()
```

Abstraction

The key features of abstraction are as follows:

- It provides you with a simple interface to the clients, where the clients can interact with class objects and call methods defined in the interface
- It abstracts the complexity of internal classes with an interface so that the client need not be aware of internal implementations

In the following example, internal details of the `Adder` class are abstracted with the `add()` method:

```
class Adder:
    def __init__(self):
        self.sum = 0
    def add(self, value):
        self.sum += value

acc = Adder()
for i in range(99):
    acc.add(i)



print(acc.sum)
```

Composition

Composition refers to the following points:

- It is a way to combine objects or classes into more complex data structures or software implementations

- In composition, an object is used to call member functions in other modules thereby making base functionality available across modules without inheritance

In the following example, the object of `class A` is composited under `class B`:

```python
class A(object):
    def a1(self):
        print("a1")

class B(object):
    def b(self):
        print("b")
        A().a1()


objectB = B()
objectB.b()
```

Object-oriented design principles

Now, let's talk about another set of concepts that are going to be crucial for us. These are nothing but the object-oriented design principles that will act as a toolbox for us while learning design patterns in detail.

The open/close principle

The open/close principle states that *classes or objects and methods should be open for extension but closed for modifications.*

What this means in simple language is, when you develop your software application, make sure that you write your classes or modules in a generic way so that whenever you feel the need to extend the behavior of the class or object, then you shouldn't have to change the class itself. Rather, a simple extension of the class should help you build the new behavior.

For example, the open/close principle is manifested in a case where a user has to create a class implementation by extending the abstract base class to implement the required behavior instead of changing the abstract class.

Advantages of this design principle are as follows:

* Existing classes are not changed and hence the chances of regression are less
* It also helps maintain backward compatibility for the previous code

The inversion of control principle

The inversion of control principle states that *high-level modules shouldn't be dependent on low-level modules; they should both be dependent on abstractions. Details should depend on abstractions and not the other way round.*

This principle suggests that any two modules shouldn't be dependent on each other in a tight way. In fact, the base module and dependent module should be decoupled with an abstraction layer in between.

This principle also suggests that the details of your class should represent the abstractions. In some cases, the philosophy gets inverted and implementation details itself decide the abstraction, which should be avoided.

Advantages of the inversion of control principle are as follows:

* The tight coupling of modules is no more prevalent and hence no complexity/rigidity in the system
* As there is a clear abstraction layer between dependent modules (provided by a hook or parameter), it's easy to deal with dependencies across modules in a better way

The interface segregation principle

As the interface segregation principle states, *clients should not be forced to depend on interfaces they don't use.*

This principle talks about software developers writing their interfaces well. For instance, it reminds the developers/architects to develop methods that relate to the functionality. If there is any method that is not related to the interface, the class dependent on the interface has to implement it unnecessarily.

For example, a `Pizza` interface shouldn't have a method called `add_chicken()`. The `Veg Pizza` class based on the `Pizza` interface shouldn't be forced to implement this method.

Advantages of this design principle are as follows:

- It forces developers to write thin interfaces and have methods that are specific to the interface
- It helps you not to populate interfaces by adding unintentional methods

The single responsibility principle

As the single responsibility principle states, *a class should have only one reason to change*.

This principle says that when we develop classes, it should cater to the given functionality well. If a class is taking care of two functionalities, it is better to split them. It refers to functionality as a reason to change. For example, a class can undergo changes because of the difference in behavior expected from it, but if a class is getting changed for two reasons (basically, changes in two functionalities), then the class should be definitely split.

Advantages of this design principle are as follows:

- Whenever there is a change in one functionality, this particular class needs to change, and nothing else
- Additionally, if a class has multiple functionalities, the dependent classes will have to undergo changes for multiple reasons, which gets avoided

The substitution principle

The substitution principle states that *derived classes must be able to completely substitute the base classes*.

This principle is pretty straightforward in the sense that it says when application developers write derived classes, they should extend the base classes. It also suggests that the derived class should be as close to the base class as possible so much so that the derived class itself should replace the base class without any code changes.

The concept of design patterns

Finally, now is the time that we start talking about design patterns! What are design patterns?

Design patterns were first introduced by **GoF** (**Gang of Four**), where they mentioned them as being solutions to given problems. If you would like to know more, GoF refers to the four authors of the book, *Design Patterns: Elements of Reusable Object-Oriented Software*. The book's authors are *Erich Gamma, Richard Helm, Ralph Johnson*, and *John Vlissides*, with a foreword by *Grady Booch*. This book covers software engineering solutions to the commonly occurring problems in software design. There were 23 design patterns first identified, and the first implementation was done with respect to the Java program language. Design patterns are discoveries and not an invention in themselves.

The key features of design patterns are as follows:

- They are language-neutral and can be implemented across multiple languages
- They are dynamic, as new patterns get introduced every now and then
- They are open for customization and hence useful for developers

Initially, when you hear about design patterns, you may feel the following:

- It's a panacea to all the design problems that you've had so far
- It's an extraordinary, specially clever way of solving a problem
- Many experts in software development world agree to these solutions
- There's something repeatable about the design, hence the word pattern

You too must have attempted to solve the problems that a design patterns intends to, but maybe your solution was incomplete, and the completeness that we're looking for is inherent or implicit in the design pattern. When we say completeness, it can refer to many factors such as the design, scalability, reuse, memory utilization, and others. Essentially, a design pattern is about learning from others' successes rather than your own failures!

Another interesting discussion that comes up on design patterns is—when do I use them? Is it in the analysis or design phase of **Software Development Life Cycle** (**SDLC**)?

Interestingly, design patterns are solutions to known issues. So they can be very much used in analysis or design, and as expected, in the development phase because of the direct relation in the application code.

Advantages of design patterns

The advantages of design patterns are as follows:

- They are reusable across multiple projects
- The architectural level of problems can be solved
- They are time-tested and well-proven, which is the experience of developers and architects
- They have reliability and dependence

Taxonomy of design patterns

Not every piece of code or design can be termed as a design pattern. For example, a programming construct or data structure that solves one problem can't be termed as a pattern. Let's understand terms in a very simplistic way below:

- **Snippet**: This is code in some language for a certain purpose, for example, DB connectivity in Python can be a code snippet
- **Design**: A better solution to solve this particular problem
- **Standard**: This is a way to solve some kind of problems, and can be very generic and applicable to a situation at hand
- **Pattern**: This is a time-tested, efficient, and scalable solution that will resolve the entire class of known issues

Context – the applicability of design patterns

To use design patterns efficiently, application developers must be aware of the context where design patterns apply. We can classify the context into the following main categories:

- **Participants**: They are classes that are used in design patterns. Classes play different roles to accomplish multiple goals in the pattern.
- **Non-functional requirements**: Requirements such as memory optimization, usability, and performance fall under this category. These factors impact the complete software solution and are thus critical.
- **Trade-offs**: Not all design patterns fit in application development as it is, and trade-offs are necessary. These are decisions that you take while using a design pattern in an application.
- **Results**: Design patterns can have a negative impact on other parts of the code if the context is not appropriate. Developers should understand the consequences and use of design patterns.

Patterns for dynamic languages

Python is a dynamic language like Lisp. The dynamic nature of Python can be represented as follows:

- Types or classes are objects at runtime.
- Variables can have type as a value and can be modified at runtime. For example, `a = 5` and `a = "John"`, the `a` variable is assigned at runtime and type also gets changed.
- Dynamic languages have more flexibility in terms of class restrictions.
- For example, in Python, polymorphism is built into the language, there are no keywords such as `private` and `protected` and everything is public by default.
- Represents a case where design patterns can be easily implemented in dynamic languages.

Classifying patterns

The book by GoF on design patterns spoke about 23 design patterns and classified them under three main categories:

- Creational patterns
- Structural patterns
- Behavioral patterns

The classification of patterns is done based primarily on how the objects get created, how classes and objects are structured in a software application, and also covers the way objects interact among themselves. Let's talk about each of the categories in detail in this section.

Creational patterns:

The following are the properties of Creational patterns:

- They work on the basis of how objects can be created
- They isolate the details of object creation
- Code is independent of the type of object to be created

An example of a creational pattern is the Singleton pattern.

Structural patterns

The following are the properties of Structural patterns:

- They design the structure of objects and classes so that they can compose to achieve larger results
- The focus is on simplifying the structure and identifying the relationship between classes and objects
- They focus on class inheritance and composition

An example of a behavior pattern is the Adapter pattern

Behavioral patterns

The following are the properties of Behavioral patterns:

- They are concerned with the interaction among objects and responsibility of objects
- Objects should be able to interact and still be loosely coupled

An example of a behavioral pattern is the Observer pattern

Summary

In this chapter, you learned about the basic concepts of object-oriented programming, such as objects, classes, variables, and features such as polymorphism, inheritance, and abstraction with code examples.

We are also now aware of object-oriented design principles that we, as developers/architects, should consider while designing an application.

Finally, we went on to explore more about design patterns and their applications and context in which they can be applied and also discussed their classifications.

At the end of this chapter, we're now ready to take the next step and study design patterns in detail.

2
The Singleton Design Pattern

In the previous chapter, we explored design patterns and their classifications. As we are aware, design patterns can be classified under three main categories: structural, behavioral, and creational patterns.

In this chapter, we will go through the Singleton design pattern—one of the simplest and well-known Creational design patterns used in application development. This chapter will give you a brief introduction to the Singleton pattern, take you through a real-world example where this pattern can be used, and explain it in detail with the help of Python implementations. You will learn about the Monostate (or Borg) design pattern that is a variant of the Singleton design pattern.

In this chapter, we will cover the following topics in brief:

- An understanding of the Singleton design pattern
- A real-world example of the Singleton pattern
- The Singleton pattern implementation in Python
- The Monostate (Borg) pattern

At the end of the chapter, we have a short summary on Singletons. This will help you think independently about some of the aspects of the Singleton design pattern.

Understanding the Singleton design pattern

Singleton provides you with a mechanism to have one, and only one, object of a given type and provides a global point of access. Hence, Singletons are typically used in cases such as logging or database operations, printer spoolers, and many others, where there is a need to have only one instance that is available across the application to avoid conflicting requests on the same resource. For example, we may want to use one database object to perform operations on the DB to maintain data consistency or one object of the logging class across multiple services to dump log messages in a particular log file sequentially.

In brief, the intentions of the Singleton design pattern are as follows:

- Ensuring that one and only one object of the class gets created
- Providing an access point for an object that is global to the program
- Controlling concurrent access to resources that are shared

The following is the UML diagram for Singleton:

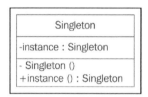

A simple way of implementing Singleton is by making the constructor private and creating a static method that does the object initialization. This way, one object gets created on the first call and the class returns the same object thereafter.

In Python, we will implement it in a different way as there's no option to create private constructors. Let's take a look at how Singletons are implemented in the Python language.

Implementing a classical Singleton in Python

Here is a sample code of the Singleton pattern in Python v3.5. In this example, we will do two major things:

1. We will allow the creation of only one instance of the Singleton class.
2. If an instance exists, we will serve the same object again.

The following code shows this:

```
class Singleton(object):
    def __new__(cls):
        if not hasattr(cls, 'instance'):
            cls.instance = super(Singleton, cls).__new__(cls)
        return cls.instance

s = Singleton()
print("Object created", s)

s1 = Singleton()
print("Object created", s1)
```

The output of the preceding snippet is given here:

```
Object created <__main__.Singleton object at 0x102078ba8>
Object created <__main__.Singleton object at 0x102078ba8>
```

In the preceding code snippet, we override the __new__ method (Python's special method to instantiate objects) to control the object creation. The s object gets created with the __new__ method, but before this, it checks whether the object already exists. The hasattr method (Python's special method to know if an object has a certain property) is used to see if the cls object has the instance property, which checks whether the class already has an object. Till the time the s1 object is requested, hasattr() detects that an object already exists and hence s1 allocates the existing object instance (located at 0x102078ba8).

Lazy instantiation in the Singleton pattern

One of the use cases for the Singleton pattern is lazy instantiation. For example, in the case of module imports, we may accidently create an object even when it's not needed. Lazy instantiation makes sure that the object gets created when it's actually needed. Consider lazy instantiation as the way to work with reduced resources and create them only when needed.

In the following code example, when we say s=Singleton(), it calls the __init__ method but no new object gets created. However, actual object creation happens when we call Singleton.getInstance(). This is how lazy instantiation is achieved.

```
class Singleton:
    __instance = None
    def __init__(self):
        if not Singleton.__instance:
```

```
            print(" __init__ method called..")
        else:
            print("Instance already created:", self.getInstance())
    @classmethod
    def getInstance(cls):
        if not cls.__instance:
            cls.__instance = Singleton()
        return cls.__instance


s = Singleton() ## class initialized, but object not created
print("Object created", Singleton.getInstance()) # Object gets created
here
s1 = Singleton() ## instance already created
```

Module-level Singletons

All modules are Singletons by default because of Python's importing behavior. Python works in the following way:

1. Checks whether a Python module has been imported.

2. If imported, returns the object for the module. If not imported, imports and instantiates it.

3. So when a module gets imported, it is initialized. However, when the same module is imported again, it's not initialized again, which relates to the Singleton behavior of having only one object and returning the same object.

The Monostate Singleton pattern

We discussed the Gang of Four and their book in *Chapter 1, Introduction to Design Patterns*. GoF's Singleton design pattern says that there should be one and only one object of a class. However, as per Alex Martelli, typically what a programmer needs is to have instances sharing the same state. He suggests that developers should be bothered about the state and behavior rather than the identity. As the concept is based on all objects sharing the same state, it is also known as the Monostate pattern.

The Monostate pattern can be achieved in a very simple way in Python. In the following code, we assign the __dict__ variable (a special variable of Python) with the __shared_state class variable. Python uses __dict__ to store the state of every object of a class. In the following code, we intentionally assign __shared_state to all the created instances. So when we create two instances, 'b' and 'b1', we get two different objects unlike Singleton where we have just one object. However, the object states, b.__dict__ and b1.__dict__ are the same. Now, even if the object variable x changes for object b, the change is copied over to the __dict__ variable that is shared by all objects and even b1 gets this change of the x setting from one to four:

```python
class Borg:
    __shared_state = {"1":"2"}
    def __init__(self):
        self.x = 1
        self.__dict__ = self.__shared_state
        pass

b = Borg()
b1 = Borg()
b.x = 4

print("Borg Object 'b': ", b) ## b and b1 are distinct objects
print("Borg Object 'b1': ", b1)
print("Object State 'b':", b.__dict__) ## b and b1 share same state
print("Object State 'b1':", b1.__dict__)
```

The following is the output of the preceding snippet:

```
Borg Object 'b':  <__main__.Borg object at 0x102078da0>
Borg Object 'b1':  <__main__.Borg object at 0x102078dd8>
Object State 'b': {'x': 4, '1': '2'}
Object State 'b1': {'x': 4, '1': '2'}
```

Another way to implement the Borg pattern is by tweaking the __new__ method itself. As we know, the __new__ method is responsible for the creation of the object instance:

```python
class Borg(object):
    _shared_state = {}
    def __new__(cls, *args, **kwargs):
        obj = super(Borg, cls).__new__(cls, *args, **kwargs)
        obj.__dict__ = cls._shared_state
        return obj
```

Singletons and metaclasses

Let's start with a brief introduction to metaclasses. A metaclass is a class of a class, which means that the class is an instance of its metaclass. With metaclasses, programmers get an opportunity to create classes of their own type from the predefined Python classes. For instance, if you have an object, MyClass, you can create a metaclass, MyKls, that redefines the behavior of MyClass to the way that you need. Let's understand them in detail.

In Python, everything is an object. If we say a=5, then type(a) returns <type 'int'>, which means a is of the int type. However, type(int) returns <type 'type'>, which suggests the presence of a metaclass as int is a class of the type type.

The definition of class is decided by its metaclass, so when we create a class with class A, Python creates it by A = type(name, bases, dict):

- name: This is the name of the class
- base: This is the base class
- dict: This is the attribute variable

Now, if a class has a predefined metaclass (by the name of MetaKls), Python creates the class by A = MetaKls(name, bases, dict).

Let's look at a sample metaclass implementation in Python 3.5:

```python
class MyInt(type):
    def __call__(cls, *args, **kwds):
        print("***** Here's My int *****", args)
        print("Now do whatever you want with these objects...")
        return type.__call__(cls, *args, **kwds)


class int(metaclass=MyInt):
    def __init__(self, x, y):
        self.x = x
        self.y = y


i = int(4,5)
```

The following is the output of the preceding code:

```
***** Here's My int ***** (4, 5)
Now do whatever you want with these objects...
```

Python's special __call__ method gets called when an object needs to be created for an already existing class. In this code, when we instantiate the int class with int(4,5), the __call__ method of the MyInt metaclass gets called, which means that the metaclass now controls the instantiation of the object. Wow, isn't this great?!

The preceding philosophy is used in the Singleton design pattern as well. As the metaclass has more control over class creation and object instantiation, it can be used to create Singletons. (Note: To control the creation and initialization of a class, metaclasses override the __new__ and __init__ method.)

The Singleton implementation with metclasses can be explained better with the following example code:

```
class MetaSingleton(type):
    _instances = {}
    def __call__(cls, *args, **kwargs):
        if cls not in cls._instances:
            cls._instances[cls] = super(MetaSingleton, \
                cls).__call__(*args, **kwargs)
        return cls._instances[cls]

class Logger(metaclass=MetaSingleton):
    pass


logger1 = Logger()
logger2 = Logger()
print(logger1, logger2)
```

A real-world scenario – the Singleton pattern, part 1

As a practical use case, we will look at a database application to show the use of Singletons. Consider an example of a cloud service that involves multiple read and write operations on the database. The complete cloud service is split across multiple services that perform database operations. An action on the UI (web app) internally will call an API, which eventually results in a DB operation.

It's clear that the shared resource across different services is the database itself. So, if we need to design the cloud service better, the following points must be taken care of:

- Consistency across operations in the database — one operation shouldn't result in conflicts with other operations

- Memory and CPU utilization should be optimal for the handling of multiple operations on the database

A sample Python implementation is given here:

```python
import sqlite3
class MetaSingleton(type):
    _instances = {}
    def __call__(cls, *args, **kwargs):
        if cls not in cls._instances:
            cls._instances[cls] = super(MetaSingleton, \
                cls).__call__(*args, **kwargs)
        return cls._instances[cls]

class Database(metaclass=MetaSingleton):
  connection = None
  def connect(self):
    if self.connection is None:
        self.connection = sqlite3.connect("db.sqlite3")
        self.cursorobj = self.connection.cursor()
    return self.cursorobj

db1 = Database().connect()
db2 = Database().connect()

print ("Database Objects DB1", db1)
print ("Database Objects DB2", db2)
```

The output of the preceding code is given here:

```
Database Objects DB1 <sqlite3.Cursor object at 0x102464570>
Database Objects DB2 <sqlite3.Cursor object at 0x102464570>
```

In the preceding code, we can see following points being covered:

1. We created a metaclass by the name of `MetaSingleton`. Like we explained in the previous section, the special `__call__` method of Python is used in the metaclass to create a Singleton.

2. The `database` class is decorated by the `MetaSingleton` class and starts acting like a Singleton. So, when the `database` class is instantiated, it creates only one object.

3. When the web app wants to perform certain operations on the DB, it instantiates the database class multiple times, but only one object gets created. As there is only one object, calls to the database are synchronized. Additionally, this is inexpensive on system resources and we can avoid the situation of memory or CPU resource.

Consider that instead of having one webapp, we have a clustered setup with multiple web apps but only one DB. Now, this is not a good situation for Singletons because, with every web app addition, a new Singleton gets created and a new object gets added that queries the database. This results in unsynchronized database operations and is heavy on resources. In such cases, database connection pooling is better than implementing Singletons.

A real-world scenario – the Singleton pattern, part 2

Let's consider another scenario where we implement health check services (such as Nagios) for our infrastructure. We create the `HealthCheck` class, which is implemented as a Singleton. We also maintain a list of servers against which the health check needs to run. If a server is removed from this list, the health check software should detect it and remove it from the servers configured to check.

In the following code, the `hc1` and `hc2` objects are the same as the class in Singleton.

Servers are added to the infrastructure for the health check with the `addServer()` method. First, the iteration of the health check runs against these servers. The `changeServer()` method removes the last server and adds a new one to the infrastructure scheduled for the health check. So, when the health check runs in the second iteration, it picks up the changed list of servers.

All this is possible with Singletons. When the servers get added or removed, the health check must be the same object that has the knowledge of the changes made to the infrastructure:

```python
class HealthCheck:
    _instance = None
    def __new__(cls, *args, **kwargs):
        if not HealthCheck._instance:
            HealthCheck._instance = super(HealthCheck, \
                cls).__new__(cls, *args, **kwargs)
        return HealthCheck._instance
    def __init__(self):
        self._servers = []
    def addServer(self):
        self._servers.append("Server 1")
        self._servers.append("Server 2")
        self._servers.append("Server 3")
        self._servers.append("Server 4")
    def changeServer(self):
        self._servers.pop()
        self._servers.append("Server 5")

hc1 = HealthCheck()
hc2 = HealthCheck()

hc1.addServer()
print("Schedule health check for servers (1)..")
for i in range(4):
    print("Checking ", hc1._servers[i])

hc2.changeServer()
print("Schedule health check for servers (2)..")
for i in range(4):
    print("Checking ", hc2._servers[i])
```

The output of the code is as follows:

```
Schedule health check for servers (1)..
Checking  Server 1
Checking  Server 2
Checking  Server 3
Checking  Server 4
Schedule health check for servers (2)..
Checking  Server 1
Checking  Server 2
Checking  Server 3
Checking  Server 5
```

Drawbacks of the Singleton pattern

While Singletons are used in multiple places to good effect, there can be a few gotchas with this pattern. As Singletons have a global point of access, the following issues can occur:

- Global variables can be changed by mistake at one place and, as the developer may think that they have remained unchanged, the variables get used elsewhere in the application.

- Multiple references may get created to the same object. As Singleton creates only one object, multiple references can get created at this point to the same object.

- All classes that are dependent on global variables get tightly coupled as a change to the global data by one class can inadvertently impact the other class.

As part of this chapter, you learned a lot on Singletons. Here are a few points that we should remember about Singletons:

- There are many real-world applications where we need to create only one object, such as thread pools, caches, dialog boxes, registry settings, and so on. If we create multiple instances for each of these applications, it will result in the overuse of resources. Singletons work very well in such situations.

- Singleton; a time-tested and proven method of presenting a global point of access without many downsides.

- Of course, there are a few downsides; Singletons can have an inadvertent impact working with global variables or instantiating classes that are resource-intensive but end up not utilizing them.

Summary

In this chapter, you learned about the Singleton design pattern and the context in which it's used. We understood that Singletons are used when there is a need to have only one object for a class.

We also looked at various ways in which Singletons can be implemented in Python. The classical implementation allowed multiple instantiation attempts but returned the same object.

We also discussed the Borg or Monostate pattern, which is a variation of the Singleton pattern. Borg allows the creation of multiple objects that share the same state unlike the single pattern described by GoF.

We went on to explore the webapp application where Singleton can be applied for consistent database operations across multiple services.

Finally, we also looked at situations where Singletons can go wrong and what situations developers need to avoid.

At the end of this chapter, we're now comfortable enough to take the next step and study other creational patterns and benefit from them.

In the next chapter, we'll take a look at another creational pattern and the Factory design pattern. We'll cover the `Factory` method and Abstract Factory patterns and understand them in the Python implementation.

3

The Factory Pattern – Building Factories to Create Objects

In the previous chapter, you learned about Singleton design patterns—what they are and how they are used in the real world along with the Python implementation. The Singleton design pattern is one of the Creational design patterns. In this chapter, we move ahead and learn about another creational pattern, the Factory pattern.

The Factory pattern is arguably the most used design pattern. In this chapter, we will understand the concept of Factory and go through the Simple Factory pattern. You will then learn about the Factory method pattern and Abstract Factory pattern with a UML diagram, real-world scenarios, and Python v3.5 implementations. We'll also compare the Factory method and Abstract Factory method.

In this chapter, we will cover the following topics in brief:

- Understanding the Simple Factory design pattern
- Discussing the Factory method and Abstract Factory method and their differences
- Implementing real-world scenarios with the Python code implementation
- Discussing the advantages and disadvantages of the patterns and their comparisons

Understanding the Factory pattern

In object-oriented programming, the term factory means a class that is responsible for creating objects of other types. Typically, the class that acts as a factory has an object and methods associated with it. The client calls this method with certain parameters; objects of desired types are created in turn and returned to the client by the factory.

So the question here really is, why do we need a factory when the client can directly create an object? The answer is, a factory provides certain advantages that are listed here:

- The first advantage is loose coupling in which object creation can be independent of the class implementation.

- The client need not be aware of the class that creates the object which, in turn, is utilized by the client. It is only necessary to know the interface, methods, and parameters that need to be passed to create objects of the desired type. This simplifies implementations for the client.

- Adding another class to the factory to create objects of another type can be easily done without the client changing the code. At a minimum, the client needs to pass just another parameter.

- The factory can also reuse the existing objects. However, when the client does direct object creation, this always creates a new object.

Let's consider the situation of a manufacturing company that manufactures toys—cars or dolls. Let's say that a machine in the company is currently manufacturing toy cars. Then, the CEO of the company feels that there is an urgent need to manufacture dolls based on the demand in the market. This situation calls for the Factory pattern. In this case, the machine becomes the interface and the CEO is the client. The CEO is only bothered about the object (or the toy) to be manufactured and knows the interface—the machine—that can create the object.

There are three variants of the Factory pattern:

- **Simple Factory pattern**: This allows interfaces to create objects without exposing the object creation logic.

- **Factory method pattern**: This allows interfaces to create objects, but defers the decision to the subclasses to determine the class for object creation.

- **Abstract Factory pattern**: An Abstract Factory is an interface to create related objects without specifying/exposing their classes. The pattern provides objects of another factory, which internally creates other objects.

The Simple Factory pattern

For some, Simple Factory is not a pattern in itself. It is more of a concept that developers need to know before they know more about the Factory method and Abstract Factory method. The Factory helps create objects of different types rather than direct object instantiation.

Let's understand this with the help of the following diagram. Here, the client class uses the Factory class, which has the `create_type()` method. When the client calls the `create_type()` method with the type parameters, based on the parameters passed, the Factory returns **Product1** or **Product2**:

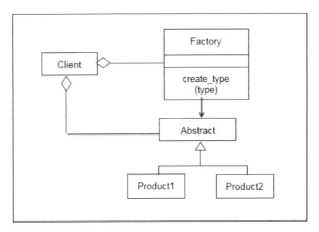

A UML Diagram of Simple Factory

Let's now understand the Simple Factory pattern with the help of a Python v3.5 code example. In the following snippet, we create an Abstract product called `Animal`. `Animal` is an abstract base class (`ABCMeta` is Python's special metaclass to make a class `Abstract`) and has the `do_say()` method. We create two products (`Cat` and `Dog`) from the Animal interface and implement `do_say()` with appropriate sounds that these animals make. `ForestFactory` is a factory that has the `make_sound()` method. Based on the type of argument passed by the client, an appropriate Animal instance is created at runtime and the right sound is printed out:

```
from abc import ABCMeta, abstractmethod

class Animal(metaclass = ABCMeta):
    @abstractmethod
    def do_say(self):
        pass

class Dog(Animal):
    def do_say(self):
        print("Bhow Bhow!!")

class Cat(Animal):
    def do_say(self):
```

```
        print("Meow Meow!!")


## forest factory defined
class ForestFactory(object):
    def make_sound(self, object_type):
        return eval(object_type)().do_say()

## client code
if __name__ == '__main__':
    ff = ForestFactory()
    animal = input("Which animal should make_sound Dog or Cat?")
    ff.make_sound(animal)
```

The following is the output of the preceding code snippet:

```
Which animal should make_sound Dog or Cat?Cat
Meow Meow!!
```

The Factory Method pattern

The following points help us understand the factory method pattern:

- We define an interface to create objects, but instead of the factory being responsible for the object creation, the responsibility is deferred to the subclass that decides the class to be instantiated.

- The Factory method creation is through inheritance and not through instantiation.

- The Factory method makes the design more customizable. It can return the same instance or subclass rather than an object of a certain type (as in the simple factory method).

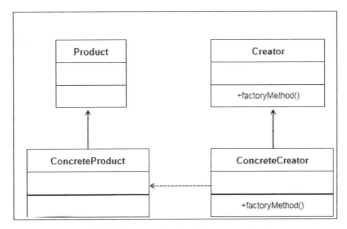

A UML diagram for the Factory method

In the preceding UML diagram, we have an abstract class, Creator, that contains factoryMethod(). The factoryMethod() method has the responsibility of creating objects of a certain type. The ConcreteCreator class has factoryMethod() that implements the Creator abstract class, and this method can change the created object at runtime. ConcreteCreator creates ConcreteProduct and makes sure that the object it creates implements the Product class and provides implementation for all the methods in the Product interface.

In brief, factoryMethod() of the Creator interface and the ConcreteCreator class decides which subclass of Product to create. Thus, the Factory method pattern defines an interface to create an object, but defers the decision ON which class to instantiate to its subclasses.

Implementing the Factory Method

Let's take a real-world scenario to understand the Factory method implementation. Consider that we would like to create profiles of different types on social networks such as LinkedIn and Facebook for a person or company. Now, each of these profiles would have certain sections. In LinkedIn, you would have a section on patents that an individual has filed or publications s/he has written. On Facebook, you'll see sections in an album of pictures of your recent visit to a holiday place. Additionally, in both these profiles, there'd be a common section on personal information. So, in brief, we want to create profiles of different types with the right sections being added to the profile.

Let's now take a look at the implementation. In the following code example, we will start by defining the `Product` interface. We will create a `Section` abstract class that defines how a section will be. We will keep it very simple and provide an abstract method, `describe()`.

We now create multiple `ConcreteProduct` classes, `PersonalSection`, `AlbumSection`, `PatentSection`, and `PublicationSection`. These classes implement the `describe()` abstract method and print their respective section names:

```python
from abc import ABCMeta, abstractmethod


class Section(metaclass=ABCMeta):
    @abstractmethod
    def describe(self):
        pass


class PersonalSection(Section):
    def describe(self):
        print("Personal Section")


class AlbumSection(Section):
    def describe(self):
        print("Album Section")


class PatentSection(Section):
    def describe(self):
        print("Patent Section")


class PublicationSection(Section):
    def describe(self):
        print("Publication Section")
```

We create a `Creator` abstract class that is named `Profile`. The `Profile` [Creator] abstract class provides a factory method, `createProfile()`. The `createProfile()` method should be implemented by `ConcreteClass` to actually create the profiles with appropriate sections. The `Profile` abstract class is not aware of the sections that each profile should have. For example, a Facebook profile should have personal information and album sections. So we will let the subclass decide this.

We create two `ConcreteCreator` classes, `linkedin` and `facebook`. Each of these classes implement the `createProfile()` abstract method that actually creates (instantiates) multiple sections (`ConcreteProducts`) at runtime:

```
class Profile(metaclass=ABCMeta):
    def __init__(self):
        self.sections = []
        self.createProfile()
    @abstractmethod
    def createProfile(self):
        pass
    def getSections(self):
        return self.sections
    def addSections(self, section):
        self.sections.append(section)


class linkedin(Profile):
    def createProfile(self):
        self.addSections(PersonalSection())
        self.addSections(PatentSection())
        self.addSections(PublicationSection())


class facebook(Profile):
    def createProfile(self):
        self.addSections(PersonalSection())
        self.addSections(AlbumSection())
```

We finally write client code that determines which `Creator` class to instantiate in order to create a profile of the desired choice:

```
if __name__ == '__main__':
    profile_type = input("Which Profile you'd like to create? 
[LinkedIn or FaceBook]")
    profile = eval(profile_type.lower())()
    print("Creating Profile..", type(profile).__name__)
    print("Profile has sections --", profile.getSections())
```

If you now run the complete code, it'll first ask you to enter the name of the profile that you'd like to create. In the following screenshot, we say `Facebook`. It then instantiates the `facebook [ConcreateCreator]` class. This internally creates `ConcreteProduct(s)`, that is, it instantiates `PersonalSection` and `AlbumSection`. If `Linkedin` is chosen, then `PersonalSection`, `PatentSection`, and `PublicationSection` are created.

The following is the output of the preceding code snippet:

```
Which Profile you'd like to create? [LinkedIn or FaceBook]FaceBook
Creating Profile.. facebook
Profile has sections -- [<__main__.PersonalSection object at 0x101988b00>, <__main__.AlbumSection object at 0x101988b38>]
```

Advantages of the Factory method pattern

As you have now learned the Factory method pattern and how to implement Factory methods, let's see the advantages of the Factory method pattern:

- It brings in a lot of flexibility and makes the code generic, not being tied to a certain class for instantiation. This way, we're dependent on the interface (Product) and not on the `ConcreteProduct` class.

- There's loose coupling, as the code that creates the object is separate from the code that uses it. The client need not bother about what argument to pass and which class to instantiate. The addition of new classes is easy and involves low maintenance.

The Abstract Factory pattern

The main objective of the Abstract Factory pattern is to provide an interface to create families of related objects without specifying the concrete class. While the factory method defers the creation of the instance to the subclasses, the goal of Abstract Factory method is to create families of related objects:

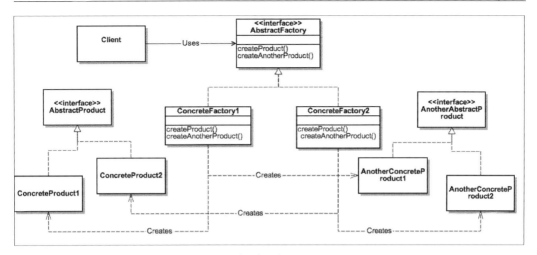

A UML Diagram for the Abstract Factory pattern

As shown in the diagram, ConcreteFactory1 and ConcreteFactory2 are created from the AbstractFactory interface. This interface has methods to create multiple products.

ConcreteFactory1 and ConcreteFactory2 implement AbstractFactory and create instances of ConcreteProduct1, ConcreteProduct2, AnotherConcreteProduct1, and AnotherConcreteProduct2.

ConcreteProduct1 and ConcreteProduct2 are in turn created from the AbstractProduct interface, and AnotherConcreteProduct1 and AnotherConcreteProduct2 are created from the AnotherAbstractProduct interface.

In effect, Abstract Factory patterns make sure that the client is isolated from the creation of objects but allowed to use the objects created. The client has the ability to access objects only through an interface. If products of one family are to be used, Abstract Factory pattern helps the client use the objects from one/ family at a time. For example, if an application under development is supposed to be platform-independent, then it needs to abstract dependencies such as OS, file system calls, among others. Abstract Factory pattern takes care of creating the required services for the entire platform so that the client doesn't have to create platform objects directly.

Implementing the Abstract Factory pattern

Consider the case of your favorite pizza place. It serves multiple types of pizzas, right? Wait, hold on, I know you want to order one right away, but let's just get back to the example for now!

Now, imagine that we create a pizza store where you are served with delicious Indian and American pizzas. For this, we first create an abstract base class, PizzaFactory (AbstractFactory in the preceding UML diagram). The PizzaFactory class has two abstract methods, createVegPizza() and createNonVegPizza(), that need to be implemented by ConcreteFactory. In this example, we create two concrete factories, namely, IndianPizzaFactory and USPizzaFactory. Look at the following code implementation for the concrete factories:

```python
from abc import ABCMeta, abstractmethod


class PizzaFactory(metaclass=ABCMeta):

    @abstractmethod
    def createVegPizza(self):
        pass

    @abstractmethod
    def createNonVegPizza(self):
        pass

class IndianPizzaFactory(PizzaFactory):

    def createVegPizza(self):
        return DeluxVeggiePizza()

    def createNonVegPizza(self):
        return ChickenPizza()


class USPizzaFactory(PizzaFactory):

    def createVegPizza(self):
        return MexicanVegPizza()

    def createNonVegPizza(self):
        return HamPizza()
```

Now, let's move ahead and define `AbstractProducts`. In the following code, we create two abstract classes, `VegPizza` and `NonVegPizza` (`AbstractProduct` and `AnotherAbstractProduct` in the preceding UML diagram]. They individually have a method defined, `prepare()` and `serve()`.

The thought process here is that vegetarian pizzas are prepared with an appropriate crust, vegetables, and seasoning, and nonvegetarian pizzas are served with nonvegetarian toppings on top of vegetarian pizzas.

We then define `ConcreteProducts` for each of the `AbstractProducts`. Now, in this case, we create `DeluxVeggiePizza` and `MexicanVegPizza` and implement the `prepare()` method. `ConcreteProducts1` and `ConcreteProducts2` would represent these classes from the UML diagram.

Later, we define `ChickenPizza` and `HamPizza` and implement the `serve()` method — these represent `AnotherConcreteProducts1` and `AnotherConcreteProducts2`:

```
class VegPizza(metaclass=ABCMeta):
    @abstractmethod
    def prepare(self, VegPizza):
        pass

class NonVegPizza(metaclass=ABCMeta):
    @abstractmethod
    def serve(self, VegPizza):
        pass

class DeluxVeggiePizza(VegPizza):
    def prepare(self):
        print("Prepare ", type(self).__name__)

class ChickenPizza(NonVegPizza):
    def serve(self, VegPizza):
        print(type(self).__name__, " is served with Chicken on ",
type(VegPizza).__name__)

class MexicanVegPizza(VegPizza):
    def prepare(self):
        print("Prepare ", type(self).__name__)

class HamPizza(NonVegPizza):
    def serve(self, VegPizza):
        print(type(self).__name__, " is served with Ham on ",
type(VegPizza).__name__)
```

When an end user approaches `PizzaStore` and asks for an American nonvegetarian pizza, `USPizzaFactory` is responsible for preparing the vegetarian pizza as the base and serving the nonvegetarian pizza with ham on top!

```python
class PizzaStore:
    def __init__(self):
        pass
    def makePizzas(self):
        for factory in [IndianPizzaFactory(), USPizzaFactory()]:
            self.factory = factory
            self.NonVegPizza = self.factory.createNonVegPizza()
            self.VegPizza = self.factory.createVegPizza()
            self.VegPizza.prepare()
            self.NonVegPizza.serve(self.VegPizza)


pizza = PizzaStore()
pizza.makePizzas()
```

The following is the output of the preceding code example:

```
Prepare  DeluxVeggiePizza
ChickenPizza  is served with Chicken on  DeluxVeggiePizza
Prepare  MexicanVegPizza
HamPizza  is served with Ham on  MexicanVegPizza
```

The Factory method versus Abstract Factory method

Now that you have learned the Factory method and Abstract Factory method, let's see the comparison of the two:

Factory method	Abstract Factory method
This exposes a method to the client to create the objects	Abstract Factory method contains one or more factory methods to create a family of related objects
This uses inheritance and subclasses to decide which object to create	This uses composition to delegate responsibility to create objects of another class
The factory method is used to create one product	Abstract Factory method is about creating families of related products

Summary

In this chapter, you learned about the Factory design pattern and the context in which it's used. We understood the basics of the Factory, and how it is effectively used in software architecture.

We looked at Simple Factory, where an appropriate instance is created at runtime based on the type of the argument passed by the client.

We also discussed the Factory method pattern, which is a variation of Simple Factory. In this pattern, we defined an interface to create objects, but the creation of objects is deferred to the subclass.

We went on to explore the Abstract Factory method, which provides an interface to create families of related objects without specifying the concrete class.

We also worked out a real-world Python implementation for all the three patterns, and compared the Factory method with Abstract Factory method.

At the end of this chapter, we're now ready to take the next step and study other types of patterns, so stay tuned.

4
The Façade Pattern – Being Adaptive with Façade

In the previous chapter, you learned about the Factory design pattern. We discussed about three variations—Simple Factory, Factory method, and Abstract Factory pattern. You also learned how each of them is used in the real world and looked at Python implementations. We also compared the Factory method with Abstract Factory patterns and listed the pros and cons. As we are now aware, both the Factory design pattern and Singleton design pattern (*Chapter 2, The Singleton Design Pattern*) are classified as Creational design patterns.

In this chapter, we will move ahead and learn about another type of design pattern, the Structural design pattern. We will get introduced to the Façade design pattern and how it is used in software application development. We will work with a sample use case and implement it in Python v3.5.

In brief, we will cover the following topics in this chapter:

- An introduction to Structural design patterns
- An understanding of the Façade design pattern with a UML diagram
- A real-world use case with the Python v3.5 code implementation
- The Façade pattern and principle of least knowledge

Understanding Structural design patterns

The following points will help us understand more about Structural patterns:

- Structural patterns describe how objects and classes can be combined to form larger structures.

- Structural patterns can be thought of as design patterns that ease the design by identifying simpler ways to realize or demonstrate relationships between entities. Entities mean objects or classes in the object-oriented world.

- While the Class patterns describe abstraction with the help of inheritance and provide a more useful program interface, Object patterns describe how objects can be associated and composed to form larger objects. Structural patterns are a combination of Class and Object patterns.

The following are a few examples of different Structural design patterns. You'd notice how each of these involve interaction between objects or classes to achieve high-level design or architectural goals.

Some of the examples of Structural design patterns are as follows:

- **Adapter pattern**: Adapting an interface to another one so that it meets the client's expectations. It tries to match interfaces of different classes based on the client's needs.

- **Bridge pattern**: This decouples an object's interface from its implementation so that both can work independently.

- **Decorator pattern**: This defines additional responsibilities for an object at runtime or dynamically. We add certain attributes to objects with an interface.

There are a few more Structural patterns that you will learn in this book. So, let's start by first taking up the Façade design pattern.

Understanding the Façade design pattern

The façade is generally referred to as the face of the building, especially an attractive one. It can be also referred to as a behavior or appearance that gives a false idea of someone's true feelings or situation. When people walk past a façade, they can appreciate the exterior face but aren't aware of the complexities of the structure within. This is how a façade pattern is used. Façade hides the complexities of the internal system and provides an interface to the client that can access the system in a very simplified way.

Consider the example of a storekeeper. Now, when you, as a customer, visit a store to buy certain items, you're not aware of the layout of the store. You typically approach the storekeeper, who is well aware of the store system. Based on your requirements, the storekeeper picks up items and hands them over to you. Isn't this easy? The customer need not know how the store looks and s/he gets the stuff done through a simple interface, the storekeeper.

The Façade design pattern essentially does the following:

- It provides a unified interface to a set of interfaces in a subsystem and defines a high-level interface that helps the client use the subsystem in an easy way.

- Façade discusses representing a complex subsystem with a single interface object. It doesn't **encapsulate** the subsystem but actually combines the underlying subsystems.

- It promotes the decoupling of the implementation with multiple clients.

A UML class diagram

We will now discuss the Façade pattern with the help of the following UML diagram:

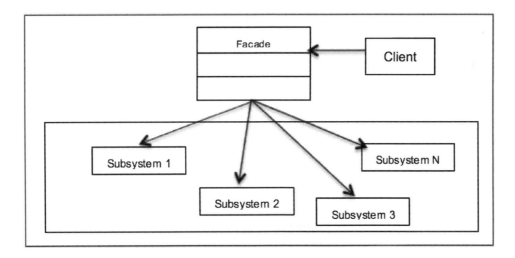

As we observe the UML diagram, you'll realize that there are three main participants in this pattern:

- **Façade**: The main responsibility of a façade is to wrap up a complex group of subsystems so that it can provide a pleasing look to the outside world.
- **System**: This represents a set of varied subsystems that make the whole system compound and difficult to view or work with.
- **Client**: The client interacts with the Façade so that it can easily communicate with the subsystem and get the work completed. It doesn't have to bother about the complex nature of the system.

You will now learn a little more about the three main participants from the data structure's perspective.

Façade

The following points will give us a better idea of Façade:

- It is an interface that knows which subsystems are responsible for a request
- It delegates the client's requests to the appropriate subsystem objects using composition

For example, if the client is looking for some work to be accomplished, it need not have to go to individual subsystems but can simply contact the interface (Façade) that gets the work done

System

In the Façade world, System is an entity that performs the following:

- It implements subsystem functionality and is represented by a class. Ideally, a System is represented by a group of classes that are responsible for different operations.
- It handles the work assigned by the Façade object but has no knowledge of the façade and keeps no reference to it.

For instance, when the client requests the Façade for a certain service, Façade chooses the right subsystem that delivers the service based on the type of service

Client

Here's how we can describe the client:

- The client is a class that instantiates the Façade
- It makes requests to the Façade to get the work done from the subsystems

Implementing the Façade pattern in the real world

To demonstrate the applications of the Façade pattern, let's take an example that we'd have experienced in our lifetime.

Consider that you have a marriage in your family and you are in charge of all the arrangements. Whoa! That's a tough job on your hands. You have to book a hotel or place for marriage, talk to a caterer for food arrangements, organize a florist for all the decorations, and finally handle the musical arrangements expected for the event.

In yesteryears, you'd have done all this by yourself, for example by talking to the relevant folks, coordinating with them, negotiating on the pricing, but now life is simpler. You go and talk to an event manager who handles this for you. S/he will make sure that they talk to the individual service providers and get the best deal for you.

Putting it in the Façade pattern perspective:

- **Client**: It's you who need all the marriage preparations to be completed in time before the wedding. They should be top class and guests should love the celebrations.
- **Façade**: The event manager who's responsible for talking to all the folks that need to work on specific arrangements such as food, and flower decorations, among others
- **Subsystems**: They represent the systems that provide services such as catering, hotel management, and flower decorations

Let's develop an application in Python v3.5 and implement this use case. We start with the client first. It's you! Remember, you're the one who has been given the responsibility to make sure that the marriage preparations are done and the event goes fine!

Let's now move ahead and talk about the Façade class. As discussed earlier, the Façade class simplifies the interface for the client. In this case, EventManager acts as a façade and simplifies the work for You. Façade talks to the subsystems and does all the booking and preparations for the marriage on your behalf. Here is the Python code for the EventManager class:

```
class EventManager(object):

    def __init__(self):
        print("Event Manager:: Let me talk to the folks\n")

    def arrange(self):
        self.hotelier = Hotelier()
        self.hotelier.bookHotel()

        self.florist = Florist()
        self.florist.setFlowerRequirements()

        self.caterer = Caterer()
        self.caterer.setCuisine()

        self.musician = Musician()
        self.musician.setMusicType()
```

Now that we're done with the Façade and client, let's dive into the subsystems. We have developed the following classes for this scenario:

- Hotelier is for the hotel bookings. It has a method to check whether the hotel is free on that day (__isAvailable).

- The Florist class is responsible for flower decorations. Florist has the setFlowerRequirements() method to be used to set the expectations on the kind of flowers needed for the marriage decoration.

- The Caterer class is used to deal with the caterer and is responsible for the food arrangements. Caterer exposes the setCuisine() method to accept the type of cuisine to be served at the marriage.

- The Musician class is designed for musical arrangements at the marriage. It uses the setMusicType() method to understand the music requirements for the event.

Let us now look at the `Hotelier` object, followed by `Florist` object and their methods:

```python
class Hotelier(object):
    def __init__(self):
        print("Arranging the Hotel for Marriage? --")

    def __isAvailable(self):
        print("Is the Hotel free for the event on given day?")
        return True

    def bookHotel(self):
        if self.__isAvailable():
            print("Registered the Booking\n\n")


class Florist(object):
    def __init__(self):
        print("Flower Decorations for the Event? --")

    def setFlowerRequirements(self):
        print("Carnations, Roses and Lilies would be used for
Decorations\n\n")


class Caterer(object):
    def __init__(self):
        print("Food Arrangements for the Event --")

    def setCuisine(self):
        print("Chinese & Continental Cuisine to be served\n\n")


class Musician(object):
    def __init__(self):
        print("Musical Arrangements for the Marriage --")

    def setMusicType(self):
        print("Jazz and Classical will be played\n\n")
```

However, you're being clever here and passing on the responsibility to the event manager, aren't you? Let's now look at the You class. In this example, you create an object of the EventManager class so that the manager can work with the relevant folks on marriage preparations while you relax.

```
class You(object):
    def __init__(self):
        print("You:: Whoa! Marriage Arrangements??!!!")
    def askEventManager(self):
        print("You:: Let's Contact the Event Manager\n\n")
        em = EventManager()
        em.arrange()
    def __del__(self):
        print("You:: Thanks to Event Manager, all preparations done!
Phew!")

you = You()
you.askEventManager()
```

The output of the preceding code is given here:

```
You:: Whoa! Marriage Arrangements??!!!
You:: Let's Contact the Event Manager


Event Manager:: Let me talk to the folks

Arranging the Hotel for Marriage? ---
Is the Hotel free for the event on given day?
Registered the Booking..


Flower Decorations for the Event? ---
Carnations, Roses and Lilies would be used for Decorations


Food Arrangements for the Event ---
Chinese & Continental Cuisine to be served


Musical Arrangements for the Marriage --
Jazz and Classical will be played


You:: Thanks to Event Manager, all preparations done! Phew!
```

We can relate to the Facade pattern with the real world scenario, in the following way:

- The `EventManager` class is the Façade that simplifies the interface for `You`

- `EventManager` uses composition to create objects of the subsystems such as `Hotelier`, `Caterer`, and others

The principle of least knowledge

As you have learned in the initial parts of the chapter, the Façade provides a unified system that makes subsystems easy to use. It also decouples the client from the subsystem of components. The design principle that is employed behind the Façade pattern is the **principle of least knowledge**.

The principle of least knowledge guides us to reduce the interactions between objects to just a few *friends* that are close enough to you. In real terms, it means the following:

- When designing a system, for every object created, one should look at the number of classes that it interacts with and the way in which the interaction happens.

- Following the principle, make sure that we avoid situations where there are many classes created that are tightly coupled to each other.

- If there are a lot of dependencies between classes, the system becomes hard to maintain. Any changes in one part of the system can lead to unintentional changes to other parts of the system, which means that the system is exposed to regressions and this should be avoided.

Frequently asked questions

Q1. What is the Law of Demeter and how is it related to the Factory pattern?

A: The Law of Demeter is a design guideline that talks about the following:

1. Each unit should have only limited knowledge of other units in the system

2. A unit should talk to its friends only

3. A unit should not know about the internal details of the object that it manipulates

The principle of least knowledge and Law of Demeter are the same and both point to the philosophy of *loose coupling*. The principle of least knowledge fits the use case of the Façade pattern as the name is intuitive and the word principle acts as a guideline, not being strict, and being useful only when needed.

Q2. Can there be multiple Façades for a subsystem?

A: Yes, one could implement more than one façade for a group of subsystem components.

Q3. What are the disadvantages of the principle of least knowledge?

A: A Façade provides a simplified interface for the clients to interact with subsystems. In the spirit of providing a simplified interface, an application can have multiple unnecessary interfaces that add to the complexity of the system and reduce runtime performance.

Q4. Can the client access the subsystems independently?

A: Yes, in fact, the Façade pattern provides simplified interfaces so that the client need not be bothered about the complexity of the subsystems.

Q5. Does the Façade add any functionality of its own?

A: A Façade can add its "thinking" to the subsystems, such as making sure that the order of innovation for subsystems can be decided by the Façade.

Summary

We began the chapter by first understanding the Structural design patterns. You then learned about the Façade design pattern and the context in which it's used. We understood the basis of Façade and how it is effectively used in software architecture. We looked at how Façade design patterns create a simplified interface for clients to use. They simplify the complexity of subsystems so that the client benefits.

The Façade doesn't encapsulate the subsystem, and the client is free to access the subsystems even without going through the Façade. You also learned the pattern with a UML diagram and sample code implementation in Python v3.5. We understood the principle of least knowledge and how its philosophy governs the Façade design patterns.

We also covered a section on FAQs that would help you get more ideas on the pattern and its possible disadvantages. We're now geared up to learn more Structural patterns in the chapters to come.

The Proxy Pattern – Controlling Object Access

In the previous chapter, we started with a brief introduction to Structural patterns and went ahead to discuss about the Façade design pattern. We understood the concept of Façade with a UML diagram and also learned how it's applied in the real world with the help of Python implementations. You learned about the upsides and downsides of the Façade pattern in the FAQs section.

In this chapter, we take a step forward and deal with the Proxy pattern that falls under the hood of the Structural design patterns. We will get introduced to the Proxy pattern as a concept and go ahead with a discussion on the design pattern and see how it is used in software application development. We will work with a sample use case and implement it in Python v3.5.

In this chapter, we will cover the following topics in brief:

- An introduction to proxy and Proxy design patterns
- A UML diagram for the Proxy pattern
- Variations of Proxy patterns
- A real-world use case with the Python v3.5 code implementation
- Advantages of the Proxy pattern
- Comparison - Façade and the Proxy pattern
- Frequently asked questions

Understanding the Proxy design pattern

Proxy, in general terms, is a system that intermediates between the seeker and provider. Seeker is the one that makes the request, and provider delivers the resources in response to the request. In the web world, we can relate this to a proxy server. The clients (users in the World Wide Web), when they make a request to the website, first connect to a proxy server asking for resources such as a web page. The proxy server internally evaluates this request, sends it to an appropriate server, and gets back the response, which is then delivered to the client. Thus, a proxy server encapsulates requests, enables privacy, and works well in distributed architectures.

In the context of design patterns, `Proxy` is a class that acts as an interface to real objects. Objects can be of several types such as network connections, large objects in memory and file, among others. In short, `Proxy` is a wrapper or agent object that wraps the real serving object. Proxy could provide additional functionality to the object that it wraps and doesn't change the object's code. The main intention of the Proxy pattern is to provide a surrogate or placeholder for another object in order to control access to a real object.

The Proxy pattern is used in multiple scenarios such as the following:

- It represents a complex system in a simpler way. For example, a system that involves multiple complex calculations or procedures should have a simpler interface that can act as a proxy for the benefit of the client.

- It adds security to the existing real objects. In many cases, the client is not allowed to access the real object directly. This is because the real object can get compromised with malicious activities. This way proxies act as a shield against malicious intentions and protect the real object.

- It provides a local interface for remote objects on different servers. A clear example of this is with the distributed systems where the client wants to run certain commands on the remote system, but the client may not have direct permissions to make this happen. So it contacts a local object (proxy) with the request, which is then executed by the proxy on the remote machine.

- It provides a light handle for a higher memory-consuming object. Sometimes, you may not want to load the main objects unless they're really necessary. This is because real objects are really heavy and may need high resource utilization. A classic example is that of profile pictures of users on a website. You're much better off showing smaller profile images in the list view, but of course, you'll need to load the actual image to show the detailed view of the user profile.

Let's understand the pattern with a simple example. Consider the example of an Actor and his Agent. When production houses want to approach an Actor for a movie, typically, they talk to the Agent and not to the Actor directly. Based on the schedule of the Actor and other engagements, the Agent gets back to the production house on the availability and interest in working in the movie. Now, in this scenario, instead of production houses directly talking to the Actor, the Agent acts as a Proxy that handles all the scheduling & payments for the Actor.

The following Python code implements this scenario where the Actor is the Proxy. The Agent object is used to find out if the Actor is busy. If the Actor is busy, the Actor().occupied() method is called and if the Actor is not busy, the Actor(). available() method gets returned.

```python
class Actor(object):
    def __init__(self):
        self.isBusy = False

    def occupied(self):
        self.isBusy = True
        print(type(self).__name__ , "is occupied with current movie")

    def available(self):
        self.isBusy = False
        print(type(self).__name__ , "is free for the movie")

    def getStatus(self):
        return self.isBusy

class Agent(object):
    def __init__(self):
        self.principal = None

    def work(self):
        self.actor = Actor()
        if self.actor.getStatus():
            self.actor.occupied()
        else:
            self.actor.available()


if __name__ == '__main__':
    r = Agent()
    r.work()
```

The Proxy design pattern essentially does the following:

- It provides a surrogate for another object so that you can control access to the original object

- It is used as a layer or interface to support distributed access

- It adds delegation and protects the real component from undesired impact

A UML class diagram for the Proxy pattern

We will now discuss the Proxy pattern with the help of the following UML diagram. As we discussed in the previous paragraph, the Proxy pattern has three main actors: the production house, Agent, and the Actor. Let's put these in a UML diagram and see how the classes look:

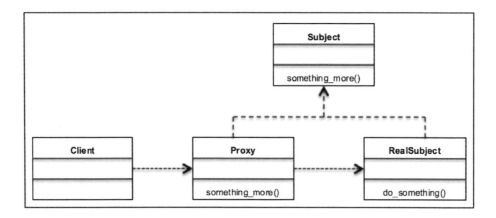

As we observe the UML diagram, you'll realize that there are three main participants in this pattern:

- Proxy: This maintains a reference that lets the Proxy access the real object. It provides an interface identical to the Subject so that Proxy can substitute the real subject. Proxies are also responsible for creating and deleting the RealSubject.

- Subject: It provides a representation for both, the RealSubject and Proxy. As Proxy and RealSubject implement Subject, Proxy can be used wherever RealSubject is expected.

- RealSubject: It defines the real object that the Proxy represents.

From the data structure's perspective, the UML diagram can be represented as follows:

- Proxy: It is a class that controls access to the RealSubject class. It handles the client's requests and is responsible for creating or deleting RealSubject.
- Subject/RealSubject: Subject is an interface that defines what RealSubject and Proxy should look like. RealSubject is an actual implementation of the Subject interface. It provides the real functionality that is then used by the client.
- Client: It accesses the Proxy class for the work to be accomplished. The Proxy class internally controls access to RealSubject and directs the work requested by Client.

Understanding different types of Proxies

There are multiple common situations where Proxies are used. We talked about some of them in the beginning of this chapter. Based on how the Proxies are used, we can categorize them as virtual proxy, remote proxy, protective proxy, and smart proxy. Let's learn a little more about them in this section.

A virtual proxy

Here, you'll learn in detail about the virtual proxy. It is a placeholder for objects that are very heavy to instantiate. For example, you want to load a large image on your website. Now this request will take a long time to load. Typically, developers will create a placeholder icon on the web page suggesting that there's an image. However, the image will only be loaded when the user actually clicks on the icon thus saving the cost of loading a heavy image in memory. Thus, in virtual proxies, the real object is created when the client first requests or accesses the object.

A remote proxy

A remote proxy can be defined in the following terms. It provides a local representation of a real object that resides on a remote server or different address space. For example, you want to build a monitoring system for your application that has multiple web servers, DB servers, celery task servers, caching servers, among others. If we want to monitor the CPU and disk utilization of these servers, we need to have an object that is available in the context of where the monitoring application runs but can perform remote commands to get the actual parameter values. In such cases, having a remote proxy object that is a local representation of the remote object would help.

A protective proxy

You'll understand more about the protective proxy with the following points. This proxy controls access to the sensitive matter object of `RealSubject`. For example, in today's world of distributed systems, web applications have multiple services that work together to provide functionality. Now, in such systems, an authentication service acts as a protective proxy server that is responsible for authentication and authorization. In this case, Proxy internally helps in protecting the core functionality of the website for unrecognized or unauthorized agents. Thus, the surrogate object checks that the caller has access permissions required to forward the request.

A smart proxy

Smart proxies interpose additional actions when an object is accessed. For example, consider that there's a core component in the system that stores states in a centralized location. Typically, such a component gets called by multiple different services to complete their tasks and can result in issues with shared resources. Instead of services directly invoking the core component, a smart proxy is built-in and checks whether the real object is locked before it is accessed in order to ensure that no other object can change it.

The Proxy pattern in the real world

We will take up a payment use case to demonstrate a real-world scenario for the Proxy pattern. Let's say that you go to shop at a mall and like a nice denim shirt there. You would like to purchase the shirt but you don't have enough cash to do so.

In yesteryears, you'd go to an ATM, take out the money, then come to the mall, and pay for it. Even earlier, you had a bank check for which you had to go to the bank, withdraw money, and then come back to pay for your expense.

Thanks to the banks, we now have something called a debit card. So now, when you want to purchase something, you present your debit card to the merchant. When you punch in your card details, the money is debited in the merchant's account for your expense.

Let's develop an application in Python v3.5 and implement the above use case. We start with the client first. You went to the shopping mall and now would like to purchase a nice denim shirt. Lets see how `Client` code is written:

- Your behavior is represented by the `You` class—the client
- To buy the shirt, the `make_payment()` method is provided by the class
- The special `__init__()` method calls the Proxy and instantiates it

- The `make_payment()` method invokes the Proxy's method internally to make the payment
- The `__del__()` method returns in case the payment is successful

Thus, the code example is as follows:

```python
class You:
    def __init__(self):
        print("You:: Lets buy the Denim shirt")
        self.debitCard = DebitCard()
        self.isPurchased = None

    def make_payment(self):
        self.isPurchased = self.debitCard.do_pay()

    def __del__(self):
        if self.isPurchased:
            print("You:: Wow! Denim shirt is Mine :-)")
        else:
            print("You:: I should earn more :(")

you = You()
you.make_payment()
```

Now let's talk about the `Subject` class. As we know, the `Subject` class is an interface that is implemented by the `Proxy` and `RealSubject`.

- In this example, the subject is the `Payment` class. It is an abstract base class and represents an interface.
- `Payment` has the `do_pay()` method that needs to be implemented by the `Proxy` and `RealSubject`.

Let's see these methods in action in the following code:

```python
from abc import ABCMeta, abstractmethod

class Payment(metaclass=ABCMeta):

    @abstractmethod
    def do_pay(self):
        pass
```

We also developed the `Bank` class that represents `RealSubject` in this scenario:

- `Bank` will actually make the payment from your account in the merchant's account.

- `Bank` has multiple methods to process the payment. The `setCard()` method is used by the `Proxy` to send the debit card details to the bank.

- The `__getAccount()` method is a private method of `Bank` that is used to get the account details of the debit card holder. For simplicity, we have enforced the debit card number to be the same as the account number.

- `Bank` also has the `__hasFunds()` method to see if the account holder has enough funds in the account to pay for the shirt.

- The `do_pay()` method that is implemented by the `Bank` class (from the Payment interface) is actually responsible for making the payment to the merchant based on available funds:

```python
class Bank(Payment):

    def __init__(self):
        self.card = None
        self.account = None

    def __getAccount(self):
        self.account = self.card # Assume card number is account
number
        return self.account

    def __hasFunds(self):
        print("Bank:: Checking if Account", self.__getAccount(),
"has enough funds")
        return True

    def setCard(self, card):
        self.card = card

    def do_pay(self):
        if self.__hasFunds():
            print("Bank:: Paying the merchant")
            return True
        else:
            print("Bank:: Sorry, not enough funds!")
            return False
```

Let's now understand the last piece, which is the `Proxy`:

- The `DebitCard` class is the `Proxy` here. When `You` wants to make a payment, it calls the `do_pay()` method. This is because `You` doesn't want go to the bank to withdraw money and pay the merchant.

- The `DebitCard` class acts as a surrogate for the `RealSubject`, `Bank`.

- The `payWithCard()` method internally controls the object creation of `RealSubject`, the `Bank` class, and presents the card details to `Bank`.

- `Bank` goes through the internal checks on the account and does the payment, as described in previous code snippet:

```python
class DebitCard(Payment):

    def __init__(self):
        self.bank = Bank()

    def do_pay(self):
        card = input("Proxy:: Punch in Card Number: ")
        self.bank.setCard(card)
        return self.bank.do_pay()
```

For a positive case, when funds are enough, the output is as follows:

```
You:: Lets buy the Denim shirt
Proxy:: Punch in Card Number: 23-2134-222
Bank:: Checking if Account 23-2134-222 has enough funds
Bank:: Paying the merchant
You:: Wow! Denim shirt is Mine :-)
```

For a negative case—insufficient funds—the output is as follows:

```
You:: Lets buy the Denim shirt
Proxy:: Punch in Card Number: 23-2134-222
Bank:: Checking if Account 23-2134-222 has enough funds
Bank:: Sorry, not enough funds!
You:: I should earn more :(
```

Advantages of the Proxy pattern

As we've seen how the Proxy pattern works in the real world, let's browse through the advantages of the Proxy pattern:

- Proxies can help improve the performance of the application by caching heavy objects or, typically, the frequently accessed objects

- Proxies also authorize the access to `RealSubject`; thus, this pattern helps in delegation only if the permissions are right

- Remote proxies also facilitate interaction with remote servers that can work as network connections and database connections and can be used to monitor systems

Comparing the Façade and Proxy patterns

Both the façade and proxy patterns are structural design patterns. They are similar in the sense that they both have a proxy/façade object in front of the real objects. Differences are really in the intent or purpose of the patterns, as shown in the following table:

Proxy pattern	Façade pattern
It provides you with a surrogate or placeholder for another object to control access to it	It provides you with an interface to large subsystems of classes
A Proxy object has the same interface as that of the target object and holds references to target objects	It minimizes the communication and dependencies between subsystems
It acts as an intermediary between the client and object that is wrapped	A Façade object provides a single, simplified interface

Frequently asked questions

Q1. What is the difference between the Decorator pattern and Proxy pattern?

A: A Decorator adds behavior to the object that it decorates at runtime, while a Proxy controls access to an object. The relationship between Proxy and `RealSubject` is at compile time and not dynamic.

Q2. What are the disadvantages of the Proxy pattern?

A: The Proxy pattern can increase the response time. For instance, if the Proxy is not well-architectured or has some performance issues, it can add to the response time of `RealSubject`. Generally, it all depends on how well a Proxy is written.

Q3. Can the client access `RealSubject` independently?

A: Yes, but there are certain advantages that Proxies provide such as virtual, remote, and others, so it's advantageous to use the Proxy pattern.

Q4. Does the Proxy add any functionality of its own?

A: A Proxy can add additional functionality to `RealSubject` without changing the object's code. Proxy and `RealSubject` would implement the same interface.

Summary

We began the chapter by understanding what Proxies are. We understood the basics of a Proxy and how it is used effectively in software architecture. You then learned about the Proxy design pattern and the context in which it's used. We looked at how the Proxy design patterns control access to the real object that provides the required functionality.

We also saw the pattern with a UML diagram and sample code implementation in Python v3.5.

Proxy patterns are implemented in four different ways: virtual proxy, remote proxy, protective proxy, and smart proxy. You learned about each of these with a real-world scenario.

We compared the Façade and Proxy design patterns so that the difference between their use cases and intentions are clear to you.

We also covered a section on FAQs that would help you get more ideas on the pattern and its possible advantages/disadvantages.

At the end of this chapter, we're now geared up to learn more Structural patterns in the chapters to come.

6

The Observer Pattern – Keeping Objects in the Know

In the previous chapter, we started with a brief introduction to Proxy and went ahead to discuss the Proxy design pattern. We understood the concept of the Proxy pattern with a UML diagram and also learned how it's applied in the real world with the help of Python implementations. You learned about the ups and downs of the Proxy pattern with the FAQ section.

In this chapter, we will talk about the third type of design pattern—the behavioral design pattern. We will be introduced to the Observer design pattern, which falls under the hood of Behavioral patterns. We will discuss how the Observer design pattern is used in software application development. We will work with a sample use case and implement it in Python v3.5.

In this chapter, we will cover the following topics in brief:

- An introduction to behavioral design patterns
- The Observer pattern and its UML diagram
- A real-world use case with the Python v3.5 code implementation
- The power of loose coupling
- Frequently asked questions

At the end of the chapter, we will summarize the entire discussion—consider this a takeaway.

Introducing Behavioral patterns

In the previous chapters of the book, you learned about creational patterns (Singleton) and structural patterns (Façade). In this section, we will get a brief idea of Behavioral patterns.

Creational patterns work on the basis of how objects can be created. They isolate the details of object creation. Code is independent of the type of object to be created. Structural patterns design the structure of objects and classes so that they can work together to achieve larger results. Their main focus is on simplifying the structure and identifying relationships between classes and objects.

Behavioral patterns, as the name suggests, focus on the responsibilities that an object has. They deal with the interaction among objects to achieve larger functionality. Behavioral patterns suggest that while the objects should be able to interact with each other, they should still be loosely coupled. We will learn about the principle of loose coupling later in this chapter.

The Observer design pattern is one of the simplest Behavioral patterns. So, let's gear up and understand more about them.

Understanding the Observer design pattern

In the Observer design pattern, an object (Subject) maintains a list of dependents (Observers) so that the Subject can notify all the Observers about the changes that it undergoes using any of the methods defined by the Observer.

In the world of distributed applications, multiple services interact with each other to perform a larger operation that a user wants to achieve. Services can perform multiple operations, but the operation they perform is directly or heavily dependent on the state of the objects of the service that it interacts with.

Consider a use case for user registration where the user service is responsible for user operations on the website. Let's say that we have another service called e-mail service that observes the state of the user and sends e-mails to the user. For example, if the user has just signed up, the user service will call a method of the e-mail service that will send an e-mail to the user for account verification. If the account is verified but has fewer credits, the e-mail service will monitor the user service and send an e-mail alert for low credits to the user.

Thus, if there's a core service in the application on which many other services are dependent, the core service becomes the Subject that has to be observed/monitored by the Observer for changes. The Observer should, in turn, make changes to the state of its own objects or take certain actions based on the changes that happen in the Subject. The above scenario, where the dependent service monitor's state changes in the core service, presents a classical case for the Observer design pattern.

In the case of a broadcast or publish/subscribe system, you'll find the usage of the Observer design pattern. Consider the example of a blog. Let's suppose that you're a tech enthusiast who loves to read about the latest articles on Python on this blog. What will you do? You subscribe to the blog. Like you, there would be multiple subscribers that are also registered with the blog. So, whenever there is a new blog, you get notified, or if there is a change on the published blog, you are also made aware of the edits. The way in which you're notified of the change can be an e-mail. Now if you apply this scenario to the Observer pattern, the blog is the Subject that maintains the list of subscribers or Observers. So when a new entry is added to the blog, all Observers are notified via e-mail or any other notification mechanism as defined by the Observer.

The main intentions of the Observer pattern are as follows:

- It defines a one-to-many dependency between objects so that any change in one object will be notified to the other dependent objects automatically
- It encapsulates the core component of the Subject

The Observer pattern is used in the following multiple scenarios:

- Implementation of the Event service in distributed systems
- A framework for a news agency
- The stock market also represents a great case for the Observer pattern

The following Python code implements the Observer design pattern:

```
class Subject:
    def __init__(self):
        self.__observers = []

    def register(self, observer):
        self.__observers.append(observer)

    def notifyAll(self, *args, **kwargs):
        for observer in self.__observers:
            observer.notify(self, *args, **kwargs)
```

```
class Observer1:
    def __init__(self, subject):
        subject.register(self)

    def notify(self, subject, *args):
        print(type(self).__name__,':: Got', args, 'From', subject)


class Observer2:
    def __init__(self, subject):
        subject.register(self)

    def notify(self, subject, *args):
        print(type(self).__name__, ':: Got', args, 'From', subject)


subject = Subject()
observer1 = Observer1(subject)
observer2 = Observer2(subject)
subject.notifyAll('notification')
```

The output of the preceding code is as follows:

```
Observer1 :: Got ('notification',) From <__main__.Subject object at 0x102178630>
Observer2 :: Got ('notification',) From <__main__.Subject object at 0x102178630>
```

A UML class diagram for the Observer pattern

Let's now understand more about the Observer pattern with the help of the
following UML diagram.

As we discussed in the previous paragraph, the Observer pattern has two main
actors: the Subject and Observer. Let's put these in a UML diagram and see how
the classes look:

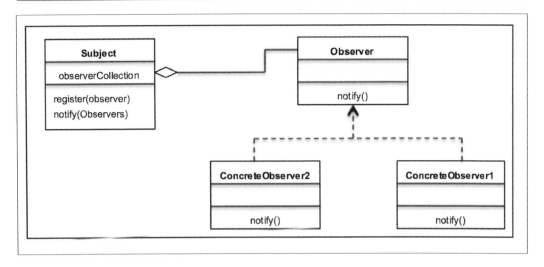

As we look at the UML diagram, you'll realize that there are three main participants in this pattern:

- Subject: The Subject class is aware of the Observer. The Subject class has methods such as register() and deregister() that are used by Observers to register themselves with the Subject class. A Subject, thus can handle multiple Observers.

- Observer: It defines an interface for objects that are observing the Subject. It defines methods that need to be implemented by the Observer to get notified of changes in the Subject.

- ConcreteObserver: It stores the state that should be consistent with that of the Subject's state. It implements the Observer interface to keep the state consistent with changes in the Subject.

The flow is straightforward. ConcreteObservers register themselves with the Subject by implementing the interface provided by the Observer. Whenever there is a change in state, the Subject notifies all ConcreteObservers with the notify method provided by the Observers.

The Observer pattern in the real world

We will take up a news agency case to demonstrate the real-world scenario for the Observer pattern. News agencies typically gather news from various locations and publish them to the subscribers. Let's look at the design considerations for this use case.

With information being sent/received in real time, a news agency should be able to publish the news as soon as possible to its subscribers. Additionally, because of the advancements in the technology industry, it's not just the newspapers, but also the subscribers that can be of different types such as an e-mail, mobile, SMS, or voice call. We should also be able to add any other type of subscriber in the future and budgeting for any new technology.

Let's develop an application in Python v3.5 and implement the preceding use case. We will start with the Subject, which is the news publisher:

- Subject behavior is represented by the `NewsPublisher` class

- `NewsPublisher` provides you with an interface so that subscribers can work with it

- The `attach()` method is used by the `Observer` to register with `NewsPublisher` and the `detach()` method helps in deregistering the `Observer`

- The `subscriber()` method returns the list of all the subscribers that have already registered with the `Subject`

- The `notifySubscriber()` method iterates over all the subscribers that have registered with `NewsPublisher`

- The `addNews()` method is used by the publisher to create new news and `getNews()` is used to return the latest news, which is then notified to the `Observer`

Let's first look at the `NewsPublisher` class:

```python
class NewsPublisher:
    def __init__(self):
        self.__subscribers = []
        self.__latestNews = None

    def attach(self, subscriber):
        self.__subscribers.append(subscriber)

    def detach(self):
        return self.__subscribers.pop()

    def subscribers(self):
        return [type(x).__name__ for x in self.__subscribers]

    def notifySubscribers(self):
        for sub in self.__subscribers:
            sub.update()
```

```
def addNews(self, news):
    self.__latestNews = news

def getNews(self):
    return "Got News:", self.__latestNews
```

Let's talk about the `Observer` interface now:

- In this example, `Subscriber` represents the `Observer`. It is an abstract base class and represents any other `ConcreteObserver`.
- `Subscriber` has the `update()` method that needs to be implemented by `ConcreteObservers`.
- The `update()` method is implemented by `ConcreteObserver` so that they get notified by the `Subject` (`NewsPublishers`) about any news getting published.

Lets us now look at the code for the `Subscriber` abstract class:

```
from abc import ABCMeta, abstractmethod

class Subscriber(metaclass=ABCMeta):

    @abstractmethod
    def update(self):
        pass
```

We also developed certain classes that represent `ConcreteObserver`:

- In this case, we have two main observers: `EmailSubscriber` and `SMSSubscriber` that implement the subscriber interface
- In addition to these two, we have another Observer, `AnyOtherObserver`, that demonstrates the loose coupling of `Observers` with the `Subject`
- The `__init__()` method of each of these `ConcreteObservers` registers them with `NewsPublisher` with the `attach()` method
- The `update()` method of `ConcreteObserver` is used internally by `NewsPublisher` to notify about the news additions

Here's how the `SMSSubscriber` class is implemented:

```
class SMSSubscriber:
    def __init__(self, publisher):
        self.publisher = publisher
        self.publisher.attach(self)
```

```
        def update(self):
            print(type(self).__name__, self.publisher.getNews())

    class EmailSubscriber:
        def __init__(self, publisher):
            self.publisher = publisher
            self.publisher.attach(self)

        def update(self):
            print(type(self).__name__, self.publisher.getNews())

    class AnyOtherSubscriber:
        def __init__(self, publisher):
            self.publisher = publisher
            self.publisher.attach(self)

        def update(self):
            print(type(self).__name__, self.publisher.getNews())
```

Now that all the required subscribers have been implemented, lets look at the
NewsPublisher and SMSSubscribers class in action:

- The client creates an object for NewsPublisher that is used by
  ConcreteObservers for various operations

- SMSSubscriber, EmailSubscriber, and AnyOtherSubscriber classes are
  initialized with publisher objects.

- In Python, when we create objects, the __init__() method gets called. In
  the ConcreteObserver class, the __init__() method internally uses the
  attach() method of NewsPublisher to register itself for news updates.

- We then print the list of all the subscribers (ConcreteObservers) that got
  registered with the Subject.

- The object of NewsPublisher (news_publisher) is then used to create new
  news with the addNews() method.

- The notifySubscribers() method of NewsPublisher is used to notify
  all subscribers of the news addition. The notifySubscribers() method
  internally calls the update() method implemented by ConcreteObservers
  so that they get the latest news.

- NewsPublisher also has the detach() method that removes the subscriber
  from the list of registered subscribers.

The following code implementation represents the interactions between the Subject
and Observers:

```
if __name__ == '__main__':
    news_publisher = NewsPublisher()
```

```
    for Subscribers in [SMSSubscriber, EmailSubscriber,
AnyOtherSubscriber]:
        Subscribers(news_publisher)
    print("\nSubscribers:", news_publisher.subscribers())

    news_publisher.addNews('Hello World!')
    news_publisher.notifySubscribers()

    print("\nDetached:", type(news_publisher.detach()).__name__)
    print("\nSubscribers:", news_publisher.subscribers())

    news_publisher.addNews('My second news!')
    news_publisher.notifySubscribers()
```

The output of the preceding code is as follows:

```
Subscribers: ['SMSSubscriber', 'EmailSubscriber', 'AnyOtherSubscriber']
SMSSubscriber ('Got News:', 'Hello World!')
EmailSubscriber ('Got News:', 'Hello World!')
AnyOtherSubscriber ('Got News:', 'Hello World!')

Detached: AnyOtherSubscriber

Subscribers: ['SMSSubscriber', 'EmailSubscriber']
SMSSubscriber ('Got News:', 'My second news!')
EmailSubscriber ('Got News:', 'My second news!')
```

The Observer pattern methods

There are two different ways of notifying the Observer of the changes that happen in the Subject. They can be classified as push or pull models.

The pull model

In the pull model, Observers play an active role as follows:

- The Subject broadcasts to all the registered Observers when there is any change
- The Observer is responsible for getting the changes or pulling data from the subscriber when there is an amendment
- The pull model is ineffective as it involves two steps—the first step where the Subject notifies the Observer and the second step where the Observer pulls the required data from the Subject

The push model

In the push model, the Subject is the one that plays a dominant role as follows:

- Unlike the pull model, the changes are pushed by the Subject to the Observer.

- In this model, the Subject can send detailed information to the Observer (even though it may not be needed). This can result in sluggish response times when a large amount of data is sent by the Subject but is never actually used by the Observer.

- Only the required data is sent from the Subject so that the performance is better.

Loose coupling and the Observer pattern

Loose coupling is an important design principle that should be used in software applications. The main purpose of loose coupling is to strive for loosely-coupled designs between objects that interact with each other. Coupling refers to the degree of knowledge that one object has about the other object that it interacts with.

Loosely-coupled designs allow us to build flexible object-oriented systems that can handle changes because they reduce the dependency between multiple objects.

The loose coupling architecture ensures following features:

- It reduces the risk that a change made within one element might create an unanticipated impact on the other elements

- It simplifies testing, maintenance, and troubleshooting problems

- The system can be easily broken down into definable elements

The Observer pattern provides you with an object design where the Subject and Observer are loosely coupled. The following points will explain this better:

- The only thing that the Subject knows about an Observer is that it implements a certain interface. It need not know the ConcreteObserver class.

- Any new Observer can be added at any point in time (as we saw in the sample example earlier in this chapter).

- The Subject need not be modified at all to add any new Observer. In the example, we saw that AnyOtherObserver can be added/removed without any changes in the Subject.

- Subjects or Observers are not tied up and can be used independently of each other. So the Observer can be reused anywhere else, if needed.

- Changes in the Subject or Observer will not affect each other. As both are independent or loosely coupled, they are free to make their own changes.

The Observer pattern – advantages and disadvantages

The Observer pattern provides you with the following advantages:

- It supports the principle of loose coupling between objects that interact with each other
- It allows sending data to other objects effectively without any change in the Subject or Observer classes
- Observers can be added/removed at any point in time

The following are the disadvantages of the Observer pattern:

- The Observer interface has to be implemented by ConcreteObserver, which involves inheritance. There is no option for composition, as the Observer interface can be instantiated.
- If not correctly implemented, the Observer can add complexity and lead to inadvertent performance issues.
- In software application, notifications can, at times, be undependable and result in race conditions or inconsistency.

Frequently asked questions

Q1. Can there be many Subjects and Observers?

A: There can be a case for a software application to have multiple Subjects and Observers. For this to work, Observers need to be notified of changes in the Subjects and which Subject underwent a change.

Q2. Who is responsible for triggering the update?

A: As you learned earlier, the Observer pattern can work in both push and pull models. Typically, the Subject triggers the update method when there are changes, but sometimes based on the application need, the **Observer** can also trigger notifications. However, care needs to be taken that the frequency should not be too high, otherwise it can lead to performance degradation, especially when the updates to the Subject are less frequent.

Q3. Can the `Subject` or `Observer` be used for access for any other use case?

A: Yes, that's the power of loose coupling that is manifested in the Observer pattern. The `Subject`/`Observer` can both be independently used.

Summary

We began the chapter by understanding the behavioral design patterns. We understood the basis of the Observer pattern and how it is effectively used in software architecture. We looked at how Observer design patterns are used to notify the `Observer` of the changes happening in the `Subject`. They manage the interaction between objects and manage one-to-many dependencies on the objects.

You also learned the pattern with a UML diagram and sample code implementation in Python v3.5.

Observer patterns are implemented in two different ways: push and pull models. You learned about each of these and discussed their implementation and performance impact.

We understood the principle of loose coupling in software design and how the Observer pattern leverages this principle in application development.

We also covered a section on FAQs that would help you get more ideas about the pattern and its possible advantages/disadvantages.

At the end of this chapter, we're now geared up to learn more Behavioral patterns in the chapters to come.

7
The Command Pattern –
Encapsulating Invocation

In the previous chapter, we started with an introduction to behavioral design patterns. You learned the concept of `Observers` and discussed the Observer design pattern. We understood the concept of the Observer design pattern with a UML diagram and also learned how it's applied in the real world with the help of Python implementations. We discussed the pros and cons of the Observer pattern. You also learned about the Observer pattern with an FAQ section and summarized the discussion at the end of the chapter.

In this chapter, we will talk about the Command design pattern. Like the Observer pattern, the Command pattern falls under the hood of Behavioral patterns. We will get introduced to the Command design pattern and discuss how it is used in software application development. We will work with a sample use case and implement it in Python v3.5.

In this chapter, we will cover the following topics in brief:

- An introduction to Command design patterns
- The Command pattern and its UML diagram
- A real-world use case with the Python v3.5 code implementation
- The Command pattern's pros and cons
- Frequently asked questions

Introducing the Command pattern

As we saw in the previous chapter, Behavioral patterns focus on the responsibilities that an object has. It deals with the interaction among objects to achieve larger functionality. The Command pattern is a behavioral design pattern in which an object is used to encapsulate all the information needed to perform an action or trigger an event at a later time. This information includes the following:

- The method name
- An object that owns the method
- Values for method parameters

Let's understand the pattern with a very simple software example. Consider the case of an installation wizard. A typical wizard may contain multiple phases or screens that capture a user's preferences. While the user browses through the wizard, s/he makes certain choices. Wizards are typically implemented with the Command pattern. A wizard is first launched with an object called the Command object. The preferences or choices made by the user in multiple phases of the wizard are then stored in the Command object. When the user clicks on the **Finish** button on the last screen of the wizard, the Command object runs an execute() method, which considers all the stored choices and runs the appropriate installation procedure. Thus, all the information regarding the choices are encapsulated in an object that can be used later to take an action.

Another easy example is that of the printer spooler. A spooler can be implemented as a Command object that stores information such as the page type (*A5-A1*), portrait/landscape, collated/non-collated. When the user prints something (say, an image), the spooler runs the execute() method on the Command object and the image is printed with the set preferences.

Understanding the Command design pattern

The Command pattern works with the following terms — Command, Receiver, Invoker, and Client:

- A Command object knows about the Receiver objects and invokes a method of the Receiver object.
- Values for parameters of the receiver method are stored in the Command object

- The invoker knows how to execute a command
- The client creates a Command object and sets its receiver

The main intentions of the Command pattern are as follows:

- Encapsulating a request as an object
- Allowing the parameterization of clients with different requests
- Allowing to save the requests in a queue (we will talk about this later in the chapter)
- Providing an object-oriented callback

The Command pattern can be used in the following multiple scenarios:

- Parameterizing objects depending on the action to be performed
- Adding actions to a queue and executing requests at different points
- Creating a structure for high-level operations that are based on smaller operations

The following Python code implements the Command design pattern. We talked about the example of the wizard earlier in the chapter. Consider that we want to develop a wizard for installation or, popularly, installer. Typically, an installation implies the copying or moving of files in the filesystem based on the choices that a user makes. In the following example, in the client code, we start by creating the Wizard object and use the preferences() method that stores the choices made by the user during various screens of the wizard. On the wizard, when **Finish** button is clicked, the execute() method is called. The execute() method picks up the preference and starts the installation:

```python
class Wizard():

    def __init__(self, src, rootdir):
        self.choices = []
        self.rootdir = rootdir
        self.src = src

    def preferences(self, command):
        self.choices.append(command)

    def execute(self):
        for choice in self.choices:
```

```
            if list(choice.values())[0]:
                print("Copying binaries --", self.src, " to ", self.
    rootdir)
            else:
                print("No Operation")


    if __name__ == '__main__':
      ## Client code
      wizard = Wizard('python3.5.gzip', '/usr/bin/')
      ## Users chooses to install Python only
      wizard.preferences({'python':True})
      wizard.preferences({'java':False})
      wizard.execute()
```

The output of the preceding code is as follows:

```
Copying binaries -- python3.5.gzip  to  /usr/bin
No Operation
```

A UML class diagram for the Command pattern

Let's now understand more about the Command pattern with the help of the following UML diagram.

As we discussed in the previous paragraph, the Command pattern has these main participants: the Command, ConcreteCommand, Receiver, Invoker, and Client. Let's put these in a UML diagram and see how the classes look:

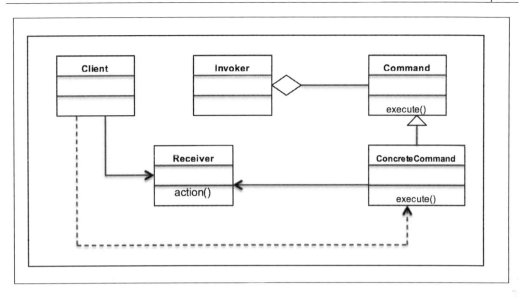

As we look at the UML diagram, you'll realize that there are five main participants in this pattern:

- Command: This declares an interface to execute an operation
- ConcreteCommand: This defines a binding between the Receiver object and action
- Client: This creates a ConcreteCommand object and sets its receiver
- Invoker: This asks ConcreteCommand to carry out the request
- Receiver: This knows how to perform the operations associated with carrying out the request

The flow is straightforward. The client asks for a command to be executed. The invoker takes the command, encapsulates it, and places it in a queue. The ConcreteCommand class is in charge of the requested command and asks the receiver to perform the given action. The following code example is to understand the pattern with all the participants involved:

```python
from abc import ABCMeta, abstractmethod

class Command(metaclass=ABCMeta):
    def __init__(self, recv):
        self.recv = recv

    def execute(self):
        pass


class ConcreteCommand(Command):
    def __init__(self, recv):
        self.recv = recv

    def execute(self):
        self.recv.action()


class Receiver:
    def action(self):
        print("Receiver Action")


class Invoker:
    def command(self, cmd):
        self.cmd = cmd

    def execute(self):
        self.cmd.execute()


if __name__ == '__main__':
    recv = Receiver()
    cmd = ConcreteCommand(recv)
    invoker = Invoker()
    invoker.command(cmd)
    invoker.execute()
```

Implementing the Command pattern in the real world

We will take up an example of the stock exchange (much talked about in the Internet world) to demonstrate the implementation of the Command pattern. What happens in a stock exchange? You, as a user of the stock exchange, create orders to buy or sell stocks. Typically, you don't buy or sell them; it's the agent or broker who plays the intermediary between you and the stock exchange. The agent is responsible for taking your request to the stock exchange and getting the work done. Imagine that you want to sell a stock on Monday morning when the exchange opens up. You can still make the request to sell stock on Sunday night to your agent even though the exchange is not yet open. The agent then queues this request to be executed on Monday morning when the exchange is open for the trading. This presents a classical case for the Command pattern.

Design considerations

Based on the UML diagram, you learned that the Command pattern has four main participants — Command, ConcreteCommand, Invoker, and Receiver. For the preceding scenario, we should create an Order interface that defines the order that a client places. We should define ConcreteCommand classes to buy or sell a stock. A class also needs to be defined for the stock exchange. We should define the Receiver class that will actually execute the trade and the agent (known as the invoker) that invokes the order and gets it executed by the receiver.

Let's develop an application in Python v3.5 and implement the preceding use case. We start with the Command object, Order:

- The Command object is represented by the Order class
- Order provides you with an interface (Python's abstract base class) so that ConcreteCommand can implement the behavior
- The execute() method is the abstract method that needs to be defined by the ConcreteCommand classes to execute the Order class

The following code represents the abstract class Order and the abstract method execute():

```
from abc import ABCMeta, abstractmethod

class Order(metaclass=ABCMeta):

    @abstractmethod
    def execute(self):
        pass
```

We have also developed certain classes that represent ConcreteCommand:

- In this case, we have two main concrete classes: BuyStockOrder and SellStockOrder that implement the Order interface
- Both the ConcreteCommand classes use the object of the stock trading system so that they can define appropriate actions for the trading system
- The execute() method of each of these ConcreteCommand classes uses the stock trade object to execute the actions to buy and sell

Let's now look at concrete classes that implement the interface:

```
class BuyStockOrder(Order):
    def __init__(self, stock):
        self.stock = stock

    def execute(self):
        self.stock.buy()


class SellStockOrder(Order):
    def __init__(self, stock):
        self.stock = stock

    def execute(self):
        self.stock.sell()
```

Now, let's talk about the stock trading system and how it's implemented:

- The StockTrade class represents the Receiver object in this example
- It defines multiple methods (actions) to execute the orders placed by ConcreteCommand objects
- The buy() and sell() methods are defined by the receiver which are called by BuyStockOrder and SellStockOrder respectively to buy or sell the stock in the exchange

Let's take a look at the `StockTrade` class:

```python
class StockTrade:
    def buy(self):
        print("You will buy stocks")

    def sell(self):
        print("You will sell stocks")
```

Another part of the implementation is the invoker:

- The `Agent` class represents the invoker.
- `Agent` is the intermediary between the client and `StockExchange` and executes the orders placed by the client.
- `Agent` defines a data member, `__orderQueue` (a list), that acts as a queue. Any new orders placed by the client are added to the queue.
- The `placeOrder()` method of Agent is responsible for queuing the orders and also executing the orders.

The following code depicts the `Agent` class which performs the role of `Invoker`:

```python
class Agent:
    def __init__(self):
        self.__orderQueue = []

    def placeOrder(self, order):
        self.__orderQueue.append(order)
        order.execute()
```

Let us now put all the above classes into perspective and look at how the client is implemented:

- The client first sets its receiver, the `StockTrade` class
- It creates orders to buy and sell stocks with `BuyStockOrder` and `SellStockOrder` (`ConcreteCommand`) that executes the action on `StockTrade`
- The invoker object is created by instantiating the `Agent` class
- The `placeOrder()` method of Agent is used to get the orders that the client places

The following is the code for the client is implemented:

```
if __name__ == '__main__':
    #Client
    stock = StockTrade()
    buyStock = BuyStockOrder(stock)
    sellStock = SellStockOrder(stock)

    #Invoker
    agent = Agent()
    agent.placeOrder(buyStock)
    agent.placeOrder(sellStock)
```

The following is the output of the preceding code:

```
You will buy stocks
You will sell stocks
```

There are multiple ways in which the Command pattern is used in software applications. We will discuss two specific implementations that are very relevant to the cloud applications:

- Redo or rollback operations:
    - While implementing the rollback or redo operations, developers can do two different things.
    - These are to create a snapshot in the filesystem or memory, and when asked for a rollback, revert to this snapshot.
    - With the Command pattern, you can store the sequence of commands, and when asked for a redo, rerun the same set of actions.

- Asynchronous task execution:
    - In distributed systems, we often need the facility to perform the asynchronous execution of tasks so that the core service is never blocked in case of more requests.
    - In the Command pattern, the invoker object can maintain a queue of requests and send these tasks to the `Receiver` object so that they can be acted on independent of the main application thread.

Advantages and disadvantages of Command patterns

The Command pattern has the following advantages:

- It decouples the classes that invoke the operation from the object that knows how to execute the operation
- It allows you to create a sequence of commands by providing a queue system
- Extensions to add a new command is easy and can be done without changing the existing code
- You can also define a rollback system with the Command pattern, for example, in the Wizard example, we could write a rollback method

The following are the disadvantages of the Command pattern:

- There are a high number of classes and objects working together to achieve a goal. Application developers need to be careful developing these classes correctly.
- Every individual command is a `ConcreteCommand` class that increases the volume of classes for implementation and maintenance.

Frequently asked questions

Q1. Can there be no `Receiver` and `ConcreteCommand` implement execute method?

A: Yes, it is definitely possible to do so. Many software applications use the Command pattern in this way too. The only thing to note here is the interaction between the invoker and receiver. If the receiver is not defined, the level of decoupling goes down; moreover, the facility to parameterize commands is lost.

Q2. What data structure do I use to implement the queue mechanism in the invoker object?

A: In the stock exchange example that we studied earlier in the chapter, we used a list to implement the queue. However, the Command pattern talks about a stack implementation that is really helpful in the case of redo or rollback development.

Summary

We began the chapter by understanding the Command design pattern and how it is effectively used in software architecture.

We looked at how Command design patterns are used to encapsulate all the information needed to trigger an event or action at a later point in time.

You also learned the pattern with a UML diagram and sample code implementation in Python v3.5 along with the explanation.

We also covered an FAQ section that would help you get more ideas on the pattern and its possible advantages/disadvantages.

We will now take up other behavioral design patterns in the chapters to come.

8
The Template Method Pattern – Encapsulating Algorithm

In the previous chapter, we started with an introduction to the Command design pattern in which an object is used to encapsulate all the information needed to perform an action or trigger an event at a later time. We understood the concept of the Command design pattern with a UML diagram and also saw how it's applied in the real world with the help of the Python implementation. We discussed the pros and cons of Command patterns, explored more in the FAQ section, and summarized the discussion at the end of the chapter.

In this chapter, we will talk about the Template design pattern, such as the Command pattern and Template pattern that falls under the hood of Behavioral patterns. We will get introduced to the Template design pattern and discuss how it is used in software application development. We will also work with a sample use case and implement it in Python v3.5.

In this chapter, we will cover the following topics in brief:

- An introduction to the Template Method design pattern
- The Template pattern and its UML diagram
- A real-world use case with the Python v3.5 code implementation
- The Template pattern – pros and cons
- The Hollywood principle, Template Method, and Template hook
- Frequently asked questions

At the end of this chapter, you will be able to analyze situations where the Template design pattern is applicable and efficiently use them to solve design-related problems. We will also summarize the entire discussion on the Template Method pattern as a takeaway.

Defining the Template Method pattern

As we saw in the previous chapter, Behavioral patterns focus on the responsibilities that an object has. It deals with the interaction among objects to achieve larger functionality. The Template Method pattern is a behavioral design pattern that defines the program skeleton or an algorithm in a method called the Template Method. For example, you could define the steps to prepare a beverage as an algorithm in a Template Method. The Template Method pattern also helps redefine or customize certain steps of the algorithm by deferring the implementation of some of these steps to subclasses. This means that the subclasses can redefine their own behavior. For example, in this case, subclasses can implement steps to prepare tea using the Template Method to prepare a beverage. It is important to note that the change in the steps (as done by the subclasses) don't impact the original algorithm's structure. Thus, the facility of overriding by subclasses in the Template Method pattern allows the creation of different behaviors or algorithms.

To talk about the Template Method pattern in software development terminology, an abstract class is used to define the steps of the algorithm. These steps are also known as *primitive operations* in the context of the Template Method pattern. These steps are defined with abstract methods, and the Template Method defines the algorithm. The ConcreteClass (that subclasses the abstract class) implements subclass-specific steps of the algorithm.

The Template Method pattern is used in the following cases:

- When multiple algorithms or classes implement similar or identical logic
- The implementation of algorithms in subclasses helps reduce code duplication
- Multiple algorithms can be defined by letting the subclasses implement the behavior through overriding

Let's understand the pattern with a very simple day-to-day example. Think of what all you do when you prepare tea or coffee. In the case of coffee, you perform the following steps to prepare the beverage:

1. Boil water.

2. Brew coffee beans.

3. Pour it in the coffee cup.

4. Add sugar and milk to the cup.

5. Stir, and the coffee is done.

Now, if you want to prepare a cup of tea, you will perform the following steps:

1. Boil water.

2. Steep the tea bag.

3. Pour the tea in a cup.

4. Add lemon to the tea.

5. Stir, and the tea is done.

If you analyze both the preparations, you will find that both the procedures are more or less the same. In this case, we can use the Template Method pattern effectively. How do we implement it? We define a `Beverage` class that has abstract methods common to preparing tea and coffee, such as `boilWater()`. We also define the `preparation()` Template Method that will call out the sequence of steps in preparing the beverage (the algorithm). We let the concrete classes, `PrepareCoffee` and `PrepareTea`, define the customized steps to achieve the goals of preparing coffee and tea. This is how the Template Method pattern avoids code duplication.

Another easy example is that of the compiler used by computer languages. A compiler essentially does two things: collects the source and compiles to the target object. Now, if we need to define a cross compiler for iOS devices, we can implement this with the help of the Template Method pattern. We will read about this example in detail later in the chapter.

Understanding the Template Method design pattern

In short, the main intentions of the Template Method pattern are as follows:

- Defining a skeleton of an algorithm with primitive operations
- Redefining certain operations of the subclass without changing the algorithm's structure
- Achieving code reuse and avoiding duplicate efforts
- Leveraging common interfaces or implementations

The Template Method pattern works with the following terms—`AbstractClass`, `ConcreteClass`, Template Method, and `Client`:

- `AbstractClass`: This declares an interface to define the steps of the algorithm
- `ConcreteClass`: This defines subclass-specific step definitions
- `template_method()`: This defines the algorithm by calling the step methods

We talked about the example of a compiler earlier in the chapter. Consider that we want to develop our own cross compiler for an iOS device and run the program.

We first develop an abstract class (compiler) that defines the algorithm of a compiler. The operations done by the compiler are collecting the source of the code written in a program language and then compiling it to get the object code (binary format). We define these steps as the `collectSource()` and `compileToObject()` abstract methods and also define the `run()` method that is responsible for executing the program. The algorithm is defined by the `compileAndRun()` method, which internally calls the `collectSource()`, `compileToObject()`, and `run()` methods to define the algorithm of the compiler. The `iOSCompiler` concrete class now implements the abstract methods and compiles/runs the Swift code on the iOS device.

> The Swift programming language is used to develop applications on the iOS platform.

The following Python code implements the Template Method design pattern:

```python
from abc import  ABCMeta, abstractmethod

class Compiler(metaclass=ABCMeta):
    @abstractmethod
    def collectSource(self):
        pass

    @abstractmethod
    def compileToObject(self):
        pass

    @abstractmethod
    def run(self):
        pass

    def compileAndRun(self):
        self.collectSource()
        self.compileToObject()
        self.run()


class iOSCompiler(Compiler):
    def collectSource(self):
        print("Collecting Swift Source Code")

    def compileToObject(self):
        print("Compiling Swift code to LLVM bitcode")

    def run(self):
        print("Program runing on runtime environment")


iOS = iOSCompiler()
iOS.compileAndRun()
```

The output of the preceding code should look as follows:

```
Collecting Swift Source Code
Compiling Swift code to LLVM bitcode
Program runing on runtime environment
```

A UML class diagram for the Template Method pattern

Let's understand more about the Template method pattern with the help of a UML diagram.

As we discussed in the previous section, the Template method pattern has the following main participants: the abstract class, concrete class, Template method, and client. Let's put these in a UML diagram and see how the classes look:

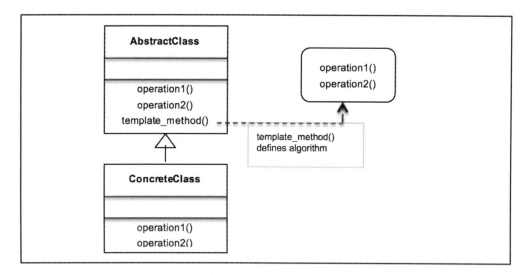

As we look at the UML diagram, you'll realize that there are four main participants in this pattern:

- `AbstractClass`: This defines the operations or steps of an algorithm with the help of abstract methods. These steps are overridden by concrete subclasses.
- `template_method()`: This defines the skeleton of the algorithm. Multiple steps as defined by abstract methods are called in the Template method to define the sequence or the algorithm itself.
- `ConcreteClass`: This implements the steps (as defined by the abstract methods) to perform subclass-specific steps of the algorithm.

The following is a code example to understand the pattern with all the participants involved:

```python
from abc import ABCMeta, abstractmethod

class AbstractClass(metaclass=ABCMeta):
    def __init__(self):
        pass

    @abstractmethod
    def operation1(self):
        pass

    @abstractmethod
    def operation2(self):
        pass

    def template_method(self):
        print("Defining the Algorithm. Operation1 follows Operation2")
        self.operation2()
        self.operation1()


class ConcreteClass(AbstractClass):

    def operation1(self):
        print("My Concrete Operation1")

    def operation2(self):
```

```
                print("Operation 2 remains same")


    class Client:
        def main(self):
            self.concreate = ConcreteClass()
            self.concreate.template_method()

    client = Client()
    client.main()
```

The output of the preceding code should look as follows:

```
Defining the Algorithm. Operation1 follows Operation2
Operation 2 remains same
My Concrete Operation1
```

The Template Method pattern in the real world

Let's take a very easy-to-understand scenario to implement the Template method pattern. Imagine the case of a travel agency, say, Dev Travels. Now how do they typically work? They define various trips to various locations and come up with a holiday package for you. A package is essentially a trip that you, as a customer, undertakes. A trip has details such as the places visited, transportation used, and other factors that define the trip itinerary. This same trip can be customized differently based on the needs of the customers. This calls for the Template Method pattern, doesn't it?

Design Considerations:

- For the preceding scenario, based on the UML diagram, we should create an `AbstractClass` interface that defines a trip
- The trip should contain multiple abstract methods that define the transportation used, places visited on `day1`, `day2`, and `day3`, assuming that it's a three-day long weekend trip, and also define the return journey

- The itinerary() Template Method will actually define the trip's itinerary
- We should define ConcreteClasses that would help us customize trips differently based on the customer's needs

Let's develop an application in Python v3.5 and implement the preceding use case. We start with the abstract class, Trip:

- The abstract object is represented by the Trip class. It is an interface (Python's abstract base class) that defines the details such as the transportation used and places to visit on different days.
- The setTransport is an abstract method that should be implemented by ConcreteClass to set the mode of transportation.
- The day1(), day2(), day3() abstract methods define the places visited on the given day.
- The itinerary() Template Method creates the complete itinerary (the algorithm, in this case, the trip). The sequence of the trip is to first define the transportation mode, then the places to visit on each day, and the returnHome.

The following code implements the scenario of Dev Travels:

```python
from abc import abstractmethod, ABCMeta

class Trip(metaclass=ABCMeta):

    @abstractmethod
    def setTransport(self):
        pass

    @abstractmethod
    def day1(self):
        pass

    @abstractmethod
    def day2(self):
        pass

    @abstractmethod
    def day3(self):
        pass
```

```
@abstractmethod
def returnHome(self):
    pass

def itinerary(self):
    self.setTransport()
    self.day1()
    self.day2()
    self.day3()
    self.returnHome()
```

We have also developed certain classes that represent the concrete class:

- In this case, we have two main concrete classes—VeniceTrip and MaldivesTrip—that implement the Trip interface

- Concrete classes represent two different trips taken by the tourists based on their choice and interests

- VeniceTrip and MaldivesTrip both implement setTransport(), day1(), day2(), day3(), and returnHome()

Let's define the concrete classes in Python code:

```
class VeniceTrip(Trip):
    def setTransport(self):
        print("Take a boat and find your way in the Grand Canal")

    def day1(self):
        print("Visit St Mark's Basilica in St Mark's Square")

    def day2(self):
        print("Appreciate Doge's Palace")

    def day3(self):
        print("Enjoy the food near the Rialto Bridge")

    def returnHome(self):
        print("Get souvenirs for friends and get back")


class MaldivesTrip(Trip):
    def setTransport(self):
```

```
        print("On foot, on any island, Wow!")

    def day1(self):
        print("Enjoy the marine life of Banana Reef")

    def day2(self):
        print("Go for the water sports and snorkelling")

    def day3(self):
        print("Relax on the beach and enjoy the sun")

    def returnHome(self):
        print("Dont feel like leaving the beach..")
```

Now, let's talk about the travel agency and tourists who want to have an awesome vacation:

- The `TravelAgency` class represents the `Client` object in this example
- It defines the `arrange_trip()` method that provides customers with the choice of whether they want to have a historical trip or beach trip
- Based on the choice made by the tourist, an appropriate class is instantiated
- This object then calls the `itinerary()` Template Method and the trip is arranged for the tourists as per the choice of the customers

The following is the implementation for the Dev travel agency and how they arrange for the trip based on the customer's choice:

```
class TravelAgency:
    def arrange_trip(self):
        choice = input("What kind of place you'd like to go historical
or to a beach?")
        if choice == 'historical':
            self.trip = VeniceTrip()
            self.trip.itinerary()
        if choice == 'beach':
            self.trip = MaldivesTrip()
            self.trip.itinerary()


TravelAgency().arrange_trip()
```

The output of the preceding code should look as follows:

```
What kind of place you'd like to go historical or to a beach?beach
On foot, on any island, Wow!
Enjoy the marine life of Banana Reef
Go for the water sports and snorkelling
Relax on the beach and enjoy the sun
Dont feel like leaving the beach..
```

If you decide to go on a historical trip, this will be the output of the code:

```
What kind of place you'd like to go historical or to a beach?historical
Take a boat and find your way in the Grand Canal
Visit St Mark's Basilica in St Mark's Square
Appreciate Doge's Palace
Enjoy the food near the Rialto Bridge
Get souvenirs for friends and get back
```

The Template Method pattern – hooks

A hook is a method that is declared in the abstract class. It is generally given a default implementation. The idea behind hooks is to give a subclass the ability to *hook into* the algorithm whenever needed. It's not imperative for the subclass to use hooks and it can easily ignore this.

For example, in the beverage example, we can add a simple hook to see if condiments need to be served along with tea or coffee based on the wish of the customer.

Another example of hook can be in the case of the travel agency example. Now, if we have a few elderly tourists, they may not want to go out on all three days of the trip as they may get tired easily. In this case, we can develop a hook that will ensure day2 is lightly loaded, which means that they can go to a few nearby places and be back with the plan of day3.

Basically, we use abstract methods when the subclass must provide the implementation, and hook is used when it is optional for the subclass to implement it.

The Hollywood principle and the Template Method

The Hollywood principle is the design principle that is summarized by *Don't call us, we'll call you*. It comes from the Hollywood philosophy where the production houses call actors if there is any role for the actor.

In the object-oriented world, we allow low-level components to hook themselves into the system with the Hollywood principle. However, the high-level components determine how the low-level systems are needed and when they are needed. In other words, high-level components treat low-level components as *Don't call us, we'll call you*.

This relates to the Template Method pattern in the sense that it's the high-level abstract class that arranges the steps to define the algorithm. Based on how the algorithm is, low-level classes are called on to define the concrete implementation for the steps.

The advantages and disadvantages of the Template Method pattern

The Template Method pattern provides you with the following advantages:

- As we saw earlier in the chapter, there is no code duplication.
- Code reuse happens with the Template Method pattern as it uses inheritance and not composition. Only a few methods need to be overridden.
- Flexibility lets subclasses decide how to implement steps in an algorithm.

The disadvantages of Template Method patterns are as follows:

- Debugging and understanding the sequence of flow in the Template Method pattern can be confusing at times. You may end up implementing a method that shouldn't be implemented or not implementing an abstract method at all. Documentation and strict error handling has to be done by the programmer.
- Maintenance of the template framework can be a problem as changes at any level (low-level or high-level) can disturb the implementation. Hence, maintenance can be painful with the Template Method pattern.

Frequently asked questions

Q1. Should a low-level component be disallowed from calling a method in a higher-level component?

A: No, a low-level component would definitely call the higher-level component through inheritance. However, what the programmer needs to make sure is that there is no circular dependency where the low-level and high-level components are dependent on each other.

Q2. Isn't the strategy pattern similar to the Template pattern?

A: The strategy pattern and Template pattern both encapsulate algorithms. Template depends on inheritance while strategy uses composition. The Template Method pattern is a compile-time algorithm selection by sub-classing while the strategy pattern is a runtime selection.

Summary

We began the chapter by understanding the Template Method design pattern and how it is effectively used in software architecture.

We also looked at how the Template Method design pattern is used to encapsulate the algorithm and provide the flexibility of implementing different behavior by overriding the methods in the subclasses.

You learned the pattern with a UML diagram and sample code implementation in Python v3.5 along with the explanation.

We also covered a section on FAQs that would help you get a better idea of the pattern and its possible advantages/disadvantages.

We will now talk about a composite pattern in the next chapter—the MVC design pattern.

9
Model-View-Controller – Compound Patterns

In the previous chapter, we started with an introduction to Template Method design pattern, in which subclasses redefine the concrete steps of the algorithm, thus achieving flexibility and code reuse. You learned about the Template Method and how it is used to construct the algorithm with a sequence of steps. We discussed the UML diagram, its pros and cons, learned more about it in the FAQ section, and summarized the discussion at the end of the chapter.

In this chapter, we will talk about Compound patterns. We will get introduced to the **Model-View-Controller** (**MVC**) design pattern and discuss how it is used in software application development. We will work with a sample use case and implement it in Python v3.5.

We will cover the following topics in brief in this chapter:

- An introduction to Compound patterns and the Model-View-Controller
- The MVC pattern and its UML diagram
- A real-world use case with the Python v3.5 code implementation
- MVC pattern — pros and cons
- Frequently asked questions

At the end of the chapter, we will summarize the entire discussion — consider this as a takeaway.

An introduction to Compound patterns

Throughout this book, we explored various design patterns. As we saw, design patterns are classified under three main categories: structural, creational, and behavioral design patterns. You also learned about each of these with examples.

However, in software implementation, patterns don't work in isolation. Every software design or solution is not implemented with just one design pattern. Actually, patterns are often used together and combined to achieve a given design solution. As GoF defines, "*a compound pattern combines two or more patterns into a solution that solves a recurring or general problem.*" A Compound pattern is not a set of patterns working together; it is a general solution to a problem.

We're now going to look at the Model-View-Controller Compound pattern. It's the best example of Compound patterns and has been used in many design solutions over the years.

The Model-View-Controller pattern

MVC is a software pattern to implement user interfaces and an architecture that can be easily modified and maintained. Essentially, the MVC pattern talks about separating the application into three essential parts: model, view, and controller. These three parts are interconnected and help in separating the ways in which information is represented to the way information is presented.

This is how the MVC pattern works: the model represents the data and business logic (how information is stored and queried), view is nothing but the representation (how it is presented) of the data, and controller is the glue between the two, the one that directs the model and view to behave in a certain way based on what a user needs. Interestingly, the view and controller are dependent on the model but not the other way round. This is primarily because a user is concerned about the data. Models can be worked with independently and this is the key aspect of the MVC pattern.

Consider the case of a website. This is one of the classical examples to describe the MVC pattern. What happens on a website? You click on a button, a few operations happen, and you get to see what you desired. How does this happen?

- You are the user and you interact with the view. The view is the web page that is presented to you. You click on the buttons on the view and it tells the controller what needs to be done.

- Controllers take the input from the view and send it to the model. The model gets manipulated based on the actions done by the user.

- Controllers can also ask the view to change based on the action it receives from the user, such as changing the buttons, presenting additional UI elements, and so on.

- The model notifies the change in state to the view. This can be based on a few internal changes or external triggers such as clicking on a button.

- The view then displays the state that it gets directly from the model. For example, if a user logs in to the website, he/she might be presented with a dashboard view (post login). All the details that need to be populated on the dashboard are given by the model to the view.

The MVC design pattern works with the following terms—Model, View, Controller and the Client:

- **Model**: This declares a class to store and manipulate data
- **View**: This declares a class to build user interfaces and data displays
- **Controller**: This declares a class that connects the model and view
- **User**: This declares a class that requests for certain results based on certain actions

The following image explains the flow of the MVC pattern:

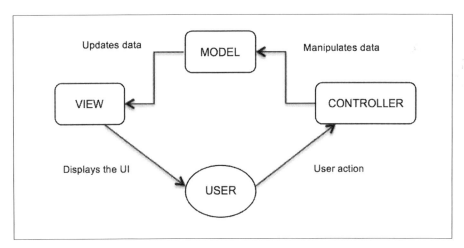

To talk about the MVC pattern in software development terminologies, let's look into the main classes involved in the MVC pattern:

- The `model` class is used to define all the operations that happen on the data (such as create, modify, and delete) and provides methods on how to use the data.

- The `view` class is a representation of the user interface. It will have methods that help us build web or GUI interfaces based on the context and need of the application. It should not contain any logic of its own and just display the data that it receives.

- The `controller` class is used to receive data from the request and send it to other parts of the system. It has methods that are used to route requests.

The MVC pattern is used in the following cases:

- When there is a need to change the presentation without changes in the business logic

- Multiple controllers can be used to work with multiple views to change the representation on the user interface

- Once again, the model can be changed without changes in the view as they can work independently of each other

In short, the main intention of the MVC pattern is as follows:

- Keeping the data and presentation of the data separate.

- Easy maintenance of the class and implementation.

- Flexibility to change the way in which data is stored and displayed. Both are independent and hence have the flexibility to change.

Let's look at the model, view, and controller in detail as covered in *Learning Python Design Patterns, Gennadiy Zlobin, Packt Publishing* as well.

Model – knowledge of the application

Model is the cornerstone of an application because it is independent of the view and controller. The view and controller in turn are dependent on the model.

Model also provides data that is requested by the client. Typically, in applications, the model is represented by the database tables that store and return information. Model has state and methods to change states but is not aware of how the data would be seen by the client.

It is critical that the model stays consistent across multiple operations; otherwise, the client may get corrupted or display stale data, which is completely undesirable.

As the model is completely independent, developers working on this piece can focus on maintenance without the need for the latest view changes.

View – the appearance

The view is a representation of data on the interface that the client sees. The view can be developed independently but should not contain any complex logic. Logic should still reside in the controller or model.

In today's world, views need to be flexible enough and should cater to multiple platforms such as desktop, mobiles, tables, and multiple screen sizes.

Views should avoid interacting directly with the databases and rely on models to get the required data.

Controller – the glue

The controller, as the name suggests, controls the interaction of the user on the interface. When the user clicks on certain elements on the interface, based on the interaction (button click or touch), the controller makes a call to the model that in turn creates, updates, or deletes the data.

Controllers also pass the data to the view that renders the information for the user to view on the interface.

The Controller shouldn't make database calls or get involved in presenting the data. The controller should act as the glue between the model and view and be as thin as possible.

Let's now get into action and develop one sample app. The Python code shown next implements the MVC design pattern. Consider that we want to develop an application that tells a user about the marketing services delivered by a cloud company, which include e-mail, SMS, and voice facilities.

We first develop the `model` class (Model) that defines the services provided by the product, namely, e-mail, SMS, and voice. Each of these services have designated rates, such as 1,000 e-mails would charge the client $2, and for 1,000 messages, the charges are $10, and $15 for 1,000 voice messages. Thus, the model represents the data about the product services and prices.

We then define the `view` class (View) that provides a method to present the information back to the client. The methods are `list_services()` and `list_pricing()`; as the name suggests, one method is used to print the services offered by the product and the other is to list the pricing for the services.

We then define the `Controller` class that defines two methods, `get_services()` and `get_pricing()`. Each of these methods queries the model and gets the data. The data is then fed to the view and thus presented to the client.

The `Client` class instantiates the controller. The `controller` object is used to call appropriate methods based on the client's request:

```python
class Model(object):
    services = {
                'email': {'number': 1000, 'price': 2,},
                'sms': {'number': 1000, 'price': 10,},
                'voice': {'number': 1000, 'price': 15,},
    }


class View(object):
    def list_services(self, services):
        for svc in services:
            print(svc, ' ')

    def list_pricing(self, services):
        for svc in services:
            print("For" , Model.services[svc]['number'],
                            svc, "message you pay $",
                        Model.services[svc]['price'])


class Controller(object):
    def __init__(self):
        self.model = Model()
        self.view = View()

    def get_services(self):
        services = self.model.services.keys()
        return(self.view.list_services(services))

    def get_pricing(self):
```

```
        services = self.model.services.keys()
        return(self.view.list_pricing(services))


class Client(object):
    controller = Controller()
    print("Services Provided:")
    controller.get_services()
    print("Pricing for Services:")
    controller.get_pricing()
```

The following is the output of the preceding code:

```
Services Provided:
sms
email
voice
Pricing for Services:
For 1000 sms message you pay $ 10
For 1000 email message you pay $ 2
For 1000 voice message you pay $ 15
```

A UML class diagram for the MVC design pattern

Let's now understand more about the MVC pattern with the help of the following UML diagram.

As we discussed in the previous sections, the MVC pattern has the following main participants: the Model, View, and Controller class.

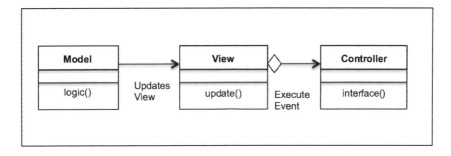

In the UML diagram, we can see three main classes in this pattern:

- The Model class: This defines the business logic or operations attached to certain tasks from the client.

- The View class: This defines the view or representation that is viewed by the client. The model presents the data to the view based on the business logic.

- The Controller class: This is essentially an interface that is between the view and model. When the client takes certain actions, the controller directs the query from the view to model.

The following is a code example to understand the pattern with all the participants involved:

```python
class Model(object):
    def logic(self):
        data = 'Got it!'
        print("Model: Crunching data as per business logic")
        return data


class View(object):
    def update(self, data):
        print("View: Updating the view with results: ", data)


class Controller(object):
    def __init__(self):
        self.model = Model()
        self.view = View()

    def interface(self):
        print("Controller: Relayed the Client asks")
        data = self.model.logic()
        self.view.update(data)


class Client(object):
    print("Client: asks for certain information")
    controller = Controller()
    controller.interface()
```

The following is the output of the preceding code:

```
Client: asks for certain information
Controller: Relayed the Cient asks
Model: Crunching data as per business logic
View: Updating the view with results:  Got it!
```

The MVC pattern in the real world

Our good old web application frameworks are based on the philosophies of MVC. Take the example of Django or Rails (Ruby): they structure their projects in the Model-View-Controller format except that it is represented as **MTV** (**Model, Template, View**) where the model is the database, templates are the views, and controllers are the views/routes.

As an example, let's take up the Tornado web application framework (http://www.tornadoweb.org/en/stable/) to develop a single-page app. This application is used to manage a user's tasks and the user has permissions to add tasks, update tasks, and delete tasks.

Let's see the design considerations:

- Let's start with the controllers first. In Tornado, controllers have been defined as views/app routes. We need to define multiple views such as listing the tasks, creating new tasks, closing the tasks, and handling an operation if a request could not be served.

- We should also define models, the database operations to list, create, or delete the tasks.

- Finally, the views are represented by templates in Tornado. Based on our app, we would need a template to show tasks, create or delete tasks, and also a template if a URL is not found.

Modules

We will use the following modules for this application:

- Torando==4.3
- SQLite3==2.6.0

Let's start by importing the Python modules in our app:

```
importtornado
import tornado.web
import tornado.ioloop
import tornado.httpserver
import sqlite3
```

The following code represents the database operations, essentially, the models in MVC. In Tornado, DB operations are performed under different handlers. Handlers perform operations on the DB based on the route requested by the user in the web app. Here, we talk about the four handlers that we have created in this example:

- IndexHandler: This returns all the tasks that are stored in the database. It returns a dictionary with key tasks. It performs the SELECT database operation to get these tasks.

- NewHandler: As the name suggests, this is useful to add new tasks. It checks whether there is a POST call to create a new task and does an INSERT operation in the DB.

- UpdateHandler: This is useful in marking a task as complete or reopening a given task. In this case, the UPDATE database operation occurs to set a task with the status as open/closed.

- DeleteHandler: This deletes a given task from the database. Once deleted, the task is no more visible in the list of tasks.

We have also developed an _execute() method that takes a SQLite query as an input and performs the required DB operation. The _execute() method does the following operations on the SQLite DB:

- Creating a SQLite DB connection
- Getting the cursor object
- Using the cursor object to make a transaction
- Committing the query
- Closing the connection

Let's look at the handlers in the Python implementation:

```
class IndexHandler(tornado.web.RequestHandler):
    def get(self):
        query = "select * from task"
```

```
        todos = _execute(query)
        self.render('index.html', todos=todos)

class NewHandler(tornado.web.RequestHandler):
    def post(self):
        name = self.get_argument('name', None)
        query = "create table if not exists task (id INTEGER \
            PRIMARY KEY, name TEXT, status NUMERIC) "
        _execute(query)
        query = "insert into task (name, status) \
            values ('%s', %d) " %(name, 1)
        _execute(query)
        self.redirect('/')

    def get(self):
        self.render('new.html')


class UpdateHandler(tornado.web.RequestHandler):
    def get(self, id, status):
        query = "update task set status=%d where \
            id=%s" %(int(status), id)
        _execute(query)
        self.redirect('/')


class DeleteHandler(tornado.web.RequestHandler):
    def get(self, id):
        query = "delete from task where id=%s" % id
        _execute(query)
        self.redirect('/')
```

If you look up these methods, you'll notice something called `self.render()`. This essentially represents the views in MVC (templates in the Tornado framework). We have three main templates:

- `index.html`: This is a template to list all the tasks

- `new.html`: This is the view to create a new task

- `base.html`: This is the base template from which other templates are inherited

Consider the following code:

```
base.html
<html>
<!DOCTYPE>
<html>
<head>
        {% block header %}{% end %}
</head>
<body>
        {% block body %}{% end %}
</body>
</html>


index.html

{% extends 'base.html' %}
<title>ToDo</title>
{% block body %}
<h3>Your Tasks</h3>
<table border="1" >
<tralign="center">
<td>Id</td>
<td>Name</td>
<td>Status</td>
<td>Update</td>
<td>Delete</td>
</tr>
    {% for todo in todos %}
<tralign="center">
<td>{{todo[0]}}</td>
<td>{{todo[1]}}</td>
            {% if todo[2] %}
<td>Open</td>
            {% else %}
<td>Closed</td>
            {% end %}
            {% if todo[2] %}
<td><a href="/todo/update/{{todo[0]}}/0">Close Task</a></td>
            {% else %}
<td><a href="/todo/update/{{todo[0]}}/1">Open Task</a></td>
            {% end %}
```

```
<td><a href="/todo/delete/{{todo[0]}}">X</a></td>
</tr>
    {% end %}
</table>

<div>
<h3><a href="/todo/new">Add Task</a></h3>
</div>
{% end %}

new.html

{% extends 'base.html' %}
<title>ToDo</title>
{% block body %}
<div>
<h3>Add Task to your List</h3>
<form action="/todo/new" method="post" id="new">
<p><input type="text" name="name" placeholder="Enter task"/>
<input type="submit" class="submit" value="add" /></p>
</form>
</div>
{% end %}
```

In Tornado, we also have the application routes that are controllers in MVC. We have four application routes in this example:

- /: This is the route to list all the tasks
- /todo/new: This is the route to create new tasks
- /todo/update: This is the route to update the task status to open/closed
- /todo/delete: This is the route to delete a completed task

The code example is as follows:

```
class RunApp(tornado.web.Application):
    def __init__(self):
        Handlers = [
                (r'/', IndexHandler),
                (r'/todo/new', NewHandler),
                (r'/todo/update/(\d+)/status/(\d+)', UpdateHandler),
```

```
        (r'/todo/delete/(\d+)', DeleteHandler),
    ]
    settings = dict(
        debug=True,
        template_path='templates',
        static_path="static",
    )
    tornado.web.Application.__init__(self, Handlers, \
        **settings)
```

We also have application settings and can start the HTTP web server to run the application:

```
if __name__ == '__main__':
    http_server = tornado.httpserver.HTTPServer(RunApp())
    http_server.listen(5000)
    tornado.ioloop.IOLoop.instance().start()
```

When we run the Python program:

1. The server gets started and runs on port 5000. The appropriate views, templates, and controllers have been configured.

2. On browsing http://localhost:5000/, we can see the list of tasks. the following screenshot shows the output in the browser:

Your Tasks

Id	Name	Status	Update	Delete
1	New Task	Open	Close Task	X
2	Wash clothes	Closed	Open Task	X
3	Cook food	Open	Close Task	X
4	Thats enough	Open	Close Task	X
5	Wow! A new Task	Open	Close Task	X

Add Task

3. We can also add a new task. Once you click on **add**, a new task gets added. In the following screenshot, a new task `Write the New Chapter` is added and listed in the task list:

When we enter the new task and click on the ADD button, the task gets added to the list of existing tasks:

Your Tasks

Id	Name	Status	Update	Delete
1	New Task	Open	Close Task	X
2	Wash clothes	Closed	Open Task	X
3	Cook food	Open	Close Task	X
4	Thats enough	Open	Close Task	X
5	Wow! A new Task	Open	Close Task	X
6	Write the New Chapter	Open	Close Task	X

Add Task

4. We can close tasks from the UI as well. For example, we update the **Cook food** task and the list gets updated. We can reopen the task if we choose to:

Your Tasks

Id	Name	Status	Update	Delete
1	New Task	Open	Close Task	X
2	Wash clothes	Closed	Open Task	X
3	Cook food	Closed	Open Task	X
4	Thats enough	Open	Close Task	X
5	Wow! A new Task	Open	Close Task	X
6	Write the New Chapter	Open	Close Task	X

5. We can also delete a task. In this case, we delete the first task, **New Task**, and the task list will get updated to remove the task:

Your Tasks

Id	Name	Status	Update	Delete
2	Wash clothes	Closed	Open Task	X
3	Cook food	Closed	Open Task	X
4	Thats enough	Open	Close Task	X
5	Wow! A new Task	Open	Close Task	X
6	Write the New Chapter	Open	Close Task	X

Benefits of the MVC pattern

The following are the benefits of the MVC pattern:

- With MVC, developers can split the software application into three major parts: model, view, and controller. This helps in achieving easy maintenance, enforcing loose coupling, and decreasing complexity.

- MVC allows independent changes on the frontend without any, or very few, changes on the backend logic, and so the development efforts can still run independently.

- On similar lines, models or business logic can be changed without any changes in the view.

- Additionally, the controller can be changed without any impact on views or models.

- MVC also helps in hiring people with specific capabilities such as platform engineers and UI engineers who can work independently in their field of expertise.

Frequently asked questions

Q1. Isn't MVC a pattern? Why is it called a Compound pattern?

A: Compound patterns are essentially groups of patterns put together to solve large design problems in software application development. The MVC pattern is the most popular and widely used Compound pattern. As it is so widely used and reliable, it is treated as a pattern itself.

Q2. Is MVC used only in websites?

A: No, a website is the best example to describe MVC. However, MVC can be used in multiple areas such as GUI applications or any other place where you need loose coupling and splitting of components in an independent way. Typical examples of MVC include blogs, movie database applications, and video streaming web apps. While MVC is useful in many places, it's overkill if you use it for the landing pages, marketing content, or quick single-page applications.

Q3. Can multiple views work with multiple models?

A: Yes, often you'd end up in a situation where the data needs to be collated from multiple models and presented in one view. One-to-one mapping is rare in today's web app world.

Summary

We began the chapter by understanding Compound patterns and looked at the Model-View-Controller pattern and how it is effectively used in software architecture. We then looked at how the MVC pattern is used to ensure loose coupling and maintain a multilayer framework for independent task development.

You also learned the pattern with a UML diagram and sample code implementation in Python v3.5 along with the explanation. We also covered a section on FAQs that would help you get more ideas on the pattern and its possible advantages/ disadvantages.

In the next chapter, we will talk about the Anti patterns. See you there!

10

The State Design Pattern

In this chapter, we will cover the State design pattern. Like the Command or Template design patterns, State pattern falls under the hood of Behavioral patterns. You will be introduced to the State design pattern, and we will discuss how it is used in software application development. We will work with a sample use case, a real-world scenario, and implement this in Python v3.5.

We will briefly cover these topics in this chapter:

- Introduction to the State design pattern
- The State design pattern and its UML diagram
- A real-world use case with the Python v3.5 code implementation
- State pattern: advantages and disadvantages

At the end of this chapter, you will appreciate the application and context of the State design pattern.

Defining the State design pattern

Behavioral patterns focus on the responsibilities that an object has. They deal with the interaction among objects to achieve larger functionality. The State design pattern is a Behavioral design pattern, which is also sometimes referred to as an **objects for states** pattern. In this pattern, an object can encapsulate multiple behaviors based on its internal state. A State pattern is also considered as a way for an object to change its behavior at runtime.

 Changing behavior at runtime is something that Python excels at!

For example, consider the case of a simple radio. A radio has AM/FM (a toggle switch) channels and a scan button to scan across multiple FM/AM channels. When a user switches on the radio, the base state of the radio is already set (say, it is set to FM). On clicking the Scan button, the radio gets tuned to multiple valid FM frequencies or channels. When the base State is now changed to AM, the scan button helps the user to tune into multiple AM channels. Hence, based on the base state (AM/FM) of the radio, the scan button's behavior dynamically changes when tuning into AM or FM channels.

Thus, the State pattern allows an object to change its behavior when its internal state changes. It will appear as though the object itself has changed its class. The State design pattern is used to develop Finite State Machines and helps to accommodate State Transaction Actions.

Understanding the State design pattern

The State design patterns works with the help of three main participants:

- State: This is considered to be an interface that encapsulates the object's behavior. This behavior is associated with the state of the object.

- ConcreteState: This is a subclass that implements the State interface. ConcreteState implements the actual behavior associated with the object's particular state.

- Context: This defines the interface of interest to clients. Context also maintains an instance of the ConcreteState subclass that internally defines the implementation of the object's particular state.

Let's take a look at the structural code implementation of the State design pattern with these three participants. In this code implementation, we define a State interface that has a Handle() abstract method. The ConcreteState classes, ConcreteStateA and ConcreteStateB, implement the State interface and, thus, define the Handle() methods specific to the ConcreteState classes. So, when the Context class is set for a state, the Handle() method of this state's ConcreteClass gets called. In the following example, since Context is set to stateA, the ConcreteStateA.Handle() method gets called and prints ConcreteStateA:

```
from abc import abstractmethod, ABCMeta

class State(metaclass=ABCMeta):

    @abstractmethod
    def Handle(self):
```

```
        pass


class ConcreteStateB(State):
    def Handle(self):
        print("ConcreteStateB")


class ConcreteStateA(State):
    def Handle(self):
        print("ConcreteStateA")


class Context(State):

    def __init__(self):
        self.state = None

    def getState(self):
        return self.state

    def setState(self, state):
        self.state = state

    def Handle(self):
        self.state.Handle()


context = Context()
stateA = ConcreteStateA()
stateB = ConcreteStateB()

context.setState(stateA)
context.Handle()
```

We will see the following output:

ConcreteStateA

Understanding the State design pattern with a UML diagram

As we saw in the previous section, there are three main participants in the UML diagram: `State`, `ConcreteState`, and `Context`. In this section, we will try to manifest them on a UML class diagram.

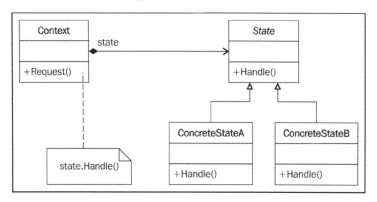

Let's understand the elements of UML diagram in detail:

- `State`: This is an interface that defines the `Handle()` abstract method. The `Handle()` method needs to be implemented by `ConcreteState`.

- `ConcreteState`: In this UML diagram, we have defined two `ConcreteClasses`: `ConcreteStateA`, and `ConcreteStateB`. These implement the `Handle()` method and define the actual action to be taken based on the `State` change.

- `Context`: This is a class that accepts the client's request. It also maintains a reference to the object's current state. Based on the request, the concrete behavior gets called.

A simple example of the State design pattern

Let's understand all three participants with a simple example. Say, we want to implement a TV remote with a simple button to perform on/off actions. If the TV is on, the remote button will switch off the TV and vice versa. In this case, the `State` interface will define the method (say, `doThis()`) to perform actions such as switching on/off the TV. We also need to define `ConcreteClass` for different states. In this example, we have two major states, `StartState` and `StopState`, which indicate when the TV is switched on and the state in which the TV is switched off, respectively.

For this scenario, the TVContext class will implement the State interface and keep a reference to the current state. Based on the request, TVContext forwards the request to ConcreteState, which implements the actual behavior (for a given state) and performs the necessary action. So, in this case, the base state is StartState (as defined earlier) and the request received by the TVContext class is to switch Off the TV. TVContext class understands the need and accordingly forwards the request to StopState concrete class which inturn calls the doThis() method to actually switch off the TV:

```python
from abc import abstractmethod, ABCMeta

class State(metaclass=ABCMeta):

    @abstractmethod
    def doThis(self):
        pass


class StartState (State):
    def doThis(self):
        print("TV Switching ON..")


class StopState (State):
    def doThis(self):
        print("TV Switching OFF..")


class TVContext(State):

    def __init__(self):
        self.state = None

    def getState(self):
        return self.state

    def setState(self, state):
        self.state = state

    def doThis(self):
        self.state.doThis()


context = TVContext()
context.getState()
```

```
start = StartState()
stop = StopState()

context.setState(stop)
context.doThis()
```

Here is the output for the preceding code:

```
TV Switching OFF..
```

The State design pattern with v3.5 implementation

Let's now take a look at a real-world use case for the State design pattern. Think of a computer system (desktop/laptop). It can have multiple states such as On, Off, Suspend, or Hibernate. Now, if we want to manifest these states with the help of State design pattern, how will we do it?

Say, we start with the ComputerState interface:

- The state should define two attributes, which are name and allowed. The name attribute represents the state of the object, and allowed is a list that defines the state's object, which it is allowed to get into.

- The state must define a switch() method, which will actually change the state of the object (in this case, the computer).

Let's take a look at the code implementation of the ComputerState interface:

```python
class ComputerState(object):
    name = "state"
    allowed = []

    def switch(self, state):
        if state.name in self.allowed:
            print('Current:',self,' => switched to new state',state.name)
            self.__class__ = state
        else:
            print('Current:',self,' => switching to',state.name,'not possible.')

    def __str__(self):
        return self.name
```

Let's now take a look at ConcreteState, which implements the State interface. We will define four states:

- On: This switches *on* the computer. The allowed states here are Off, Suspend, and Hibernate.

- Off: This switches *off* the computer. The allowed state here is just On.

- Hibernate: This state puts the computer in the *hibernate* mode. The computer can only get switched on when it's in this state.

- Suspend: This state *suspends* the computer, and once the computer is suspended, it can be switched on.

Let's now take a look at the code:

```
class Off(ComputerState):
    name = "off"
    allowed = ['on']

class On(ComputerState):
    name = "on"
    allowed = ['off','suspend','hibernate']

class Suspend(ComputerState):
    name = "suspend"
    allowed = ['on']

class Hibernate(ComputerState):
    name = "hibernate"
    allowed = ['on']
```

Now, we explore the context class (Computer). The context does two main things:

- __init__(): This method defines the base state of the computer

- change(): This method will change the state of the object, and the actual change in behavior is implemented by the ConcreteState classes (on, off, suspend, and hibernate)

Here is the implementation of the preceding methods:

```
class Computer(object):
    def __init__(self, model='HP'):
        self.model = model
        self.state = Off()

    def change(self, state):
        self.state.switch(state)
```

The following is the code for the client. We create the object of the Computer class (Context) and pass a state to it. The state can be either of these: On, Off, Suspend, and Hibernate. Based on the new state, the context calls its change(state) method, which eventually switches the actual state of the computer:

```python
if __name__ == "__main__":
    comp = Computer()
    # Switch on
    comp.change(On)
    # Switch off
    comp.change(Off)

    # Switch on again
    comp.change(On)
    # Suspend
    comp.change(Suspend)
    # Try to hibernate - cannot!
    comp.change(Hibernate)
    # switch on back
    comp.change(On)
    # Finally off
    comp.change(Off)
```

Now, we can observe the following output:

```
Current: off  => switched to new state on
Current: on  => switched to new state off
Current: off  => switched to new state on
Current: on  => switched to new state suspend
Current: suspend  => switching to hibernate not possible
Current: suspend  => switched to new state on
Current: on  => switched to new state off
```

__class__ is a built-in attribute of every class. It is a reference to the class. For instance, self.__class__.__name__ represents the name of the class. In this example, we use __class__ attribute of Python to change the State. So, when we pass the state to the change() method, the class of the objects gets dynamically changed at runtime. The comp.change(On) code, changes the object state to On and subsequently to different states like Suspend, Hibernate, and Off.

Advantages/disadvantages of the State pattern

Here are the benefits of the State design pattern:

- In the State design pattern, an object's behavior is the result of the function of its state, and the behavior gets changed at runtime depending on the state. This removes the dependency on the if/else or switch/case conditional logic. For example, in the TV remote scenario, we could have also implemented the behavior by simply writing one class and method that will ask for a parameter and perform an action (switch the TV on/off) with an `if/else` block.

- With State pattern, the benefits of implementing polymorphic behavior are evident, and it is also easier to add states to support additional behavior.

- The State design pattern also improves **Cohesion** since state-specific behaviors are aggregated into the `ConcreteState` classes, which are placed in one location in the code.

- With the State design pattern, it is very easy to add a behavior by just adding one more `ConcreteState` class. State pattern thus improves the flexibility to extend the behavior of the application and overall improves code maintenance.

We have seen the advantages of state patterns. However, they also have a few pitfalls:

- **Class Explosion**: Since every state needs to be defined with the help of `ConcreteState`, there is a chance that we might end up writing many more classes with a small functionality. Consider the case of finite state machines—if there are many states but each state is not too different from another state, we'd still need to write them as separate `ConcreteState` classes. This increases the amount of code we need to write, and it becomes difficult to review the structure of a state machine.

- With the introduction of every new behavior (even though adding behavior is just adding one more `ConcreteState`), the `Context` class needs to be updated to deal with each behavior. This makes the `Context` behavior more brittle with every new behavior.

Summary

To summarize what we've learned so far, in State design patterns, the object's behavior is decided based on its state. The state of the object can be changed at runtime. Python's ability to change behavior at runtime makes it very easy to apply and implement the State design pattern. The State pattern also gives us control over deciding the states that objects can take up such as those in the computer example that we saw earlier in the chapter. The `Context` class provides an easier interface for clients, and `ConcreteState` makes sure it is easy to add behaviors to the objects. Thus, the State pattern improves cohesion, flexibility to extend, and removes redundant code blocks. We academically studied the pattern in the form of a UML diagram and learned about the implementation aspects of the State pattern with help of the Python v3.5 code implementation. We also took a look at the few pitfalls you might encounter when it comes to the State pattern, and the code which can significantly increase when it comes to adding more states or behaviors. I hope you had a nice time going through this chapter!

11
AntiPatterns

In the previous chapter, we started with an introduction to Compound patterns. You learned how design patterns work together to solve a real-world design problem. We went further to explore the Model-View-Controller design pattern—the king of Compound patterns. We understood that the MVC pattern is used when we need loose coupling between components and separation of the way in which data is stored from the way data is presented. We also went through the UML diagram of the MVC pattern and read about how the individual components (model, view, and controller) work among themselves. We also saw how it's applied in the real world with the help of the Python implementation. We discussed the benefits of the MVC pattern, learned more about it in the FAQs section, and summarized the discussion at the end of chapter.

In this chapter, we will talk about AntiPatterns. This is different from all the other chapters in the book; here, we will cover what we shouldn't do as architects or software engineers. We will understand what AntiPatterns are and how they are visible in software design or development aspects with the help of theoretical and practical examples.

In brief, we will cover the following topics in this chapter:

- An introduction to AntiPatterns
- AntiPatterns with examples
- Common pitfalls during development

At the end of the chapter, we will summarize the entire discussion—consider this as a takeaway.

An introduction to AntiPatterns

Software design principles represent a set of rules or guidelines that help software developers make design-level decisions. According to Robert Martin, there are four aspects of a bad design:

- **Immobile**: An application is developed in such a way that it becomes very hard to reuse

- **Rigid**: An application is developed in such a manner that any small change may in turn result in moving of too many parts of the software

- **Fragile**: Any change in the current application results in breaking the existing system fairly easily

- **Viscose**: Changes are done by the developer in the code or environment itself to avoid difficult architectural level changes

The above aspects of bad design, if applied, result in solutions that should not be implemented in the software architecture or development.

An AntiPattern is an outcome of a solution to recurring problems so that the outcome is ineffective and becomes counterproductive. What does this mean? Let's say that you come across a software design problem. You get down to solving this problem. However, what if the solution has a negative impact on the design or causes any performance issues in the application? Hence, AntiPatterns are common defective processes and implementations within software applications.

AntiPatterns may be the result of the following:

- A developer not knowing the software development practices

- A developer not applying design patterns in the correct context

AntiPatterns can prove beneficial as they provide an opportunity for the following reasons:

- Recognize recurring problems in the software industry and provide a detailed remedy for most of these issues

- Develop tools to recognize these problems and determine the underlying causes

- Describe the measures that can be taken at several levels of improving the application and architecture

AntiPatterns can be classified under two main categories:

1. Software development AntiPatterns
2. Software architecture AntiPatterns

Software development AntiPatterns

When you start software development for an application or project, you think of the code structure. This structure is consistent with the product architecture, design, customer use cases, and many other development considerations.

Often, when the software is developed, it gets deviated from the original code structure due to the following reasons:

- The thought process of the developer evolves with development
- Use cases tend to change based on customer feedback
- Data structures designed initially may undergo change with functionality or scalability considerations

Due to the preceding reasons, software often undergoes refactoring. Refactoring is taken with a negative connotation by many, but in reality, refactoring is one of the critical parts of the software development journey, which provides developers an opportunity to relook the data structures and think about scalability and ever-evolving customer's needs.

The following examples provide you with an overview of different AntiPatterns observed in software development and architecture. We will cover only a few of them along with causes, symptoms, and consequences.

Spaghetti code

This is the most common and most heard of AntiPattern in software development. Do you know how spaghetti looks? So complicated, isn't it? Software control flows also get tangled if structures are developed in an ad hoc manner. Spaghetti code is difficult to maintain and optimize.

The typical causes of Spaghetti include the following:

- Ignorance on object-oriented programming and analysis
- Product architecture or design that is not considered
- Quick fix mentality

You know you're stuck with Spaghetti when the following points are true:

- Minimum reuse of structures is possible
- Maintenance efforts are too high
- Extension and flexibility to change is reduced

Golden Hammer

In the software industry, you would have seen many examples where a given solution (technology, design, or module) is used in many places because the solution would have yielded benefits in multiple projects. As we have seen with examples throughout this book, a solution is best suited in a given context and applied to certain types of problems. However, teams or software developers tend to go with one proven solution irrespective of whether it suits the need. This is the reason that it's called Golden Hammer, a hammer for all the nails possible (a solution to all problems).

The typical causes of Golden Hammer include the following:

- It comes as a recommendation from the top (architects or technology leaders) who are not close to the given problem at hand
- A solution has yielded a lot of benefits in the past but in projects with a different context and requirements
- A company is stuck with this technology as they have invested money in training the staff or the staff is comfortable with it

The consequences of a Golden Hammer are as follows:

- One solution is obsessively applied to all software projects
- The product is described, not by the features, but the technology used in development
- In the company corridors, you hear developers talking, "That could have been better than using this."
- Requirements are not completed and not in sync with user expectations

Lava Flow

This AntiPattern is related to Dead Code, or an unusable piece of code, lying in the software application for the fear of breaking something else if it is modified. As more time passes, this piece of code continues to remain in the software and solidifies its position, like lava turning into a hard rock. It may happen in cases where you start developing software to support a certain use case but the use case itself changes with time.

The causes of a Lava Flow include the following:

- A lot of trial and error code in the production
- Single-handedly written code that is not reviewed and is handed over to other development teams without any training
- The initial thought of the software architecture or design is implemented in the code base, but no one understands it anymore

The symptoms of a Lava Flow are as follows:

- Low code coverage (if at all done) for developed tests
- A lot of occurrences of commented code without reasons
- Obsolete interfaces, or developers try to work around existing code

Copy-and-paste or cut-and-paste programming

As you know, this is one of the most common AntiPatterns. Experienced developers put their code snippets online (GitHub or Stack Overflow) that are solutions to some commonly occurring issues. Developers often copy these snippets as is and use in their application to move further in the application development. In this case, there is no validation that this is the most optimized code or even that the code actually fits the context. This leads to inflexible software application that is hard to maintain.

The causes of copy-and-paste or cut-and-paste are as follows:

- Novice developers not used to writing code or not aware how to develop
- Quick bug fix or moving forward with development
- Code duplication for need of a code structure or standardization across modules
- A lack of long-term thinking or forethought

The consequences of cut-and-paste or copy-and-paste include the following:

- Similar type of issues across software application
- Higher maintenance costs and increased bug life cycle
- Less modular code base with the same code running into a number of lines
- Inheriting issues that existed in the first place

Software architecture AntiPatterns

Software architecture is an important piece of overall system architecture. While system architecture focuses on aspects such as the design, tools, and hardware among other things, software architecture looks at modeling the software that is well understood by the development and test teams, product managers, and other stakeholders. This architecture plays a critical role in determining the success of the implementation and how the product works for the customers.

We will discuss some of the architecture-level AntiPatterns that we observe in the real world with development and implementation software architecture.

Reinventing the wheel

We often hear technology leaders talking about NOT reinventing the wheel. What does it essentially mean? For some, this may mean code or library reuse. Actually, it points to architecture reuse. For example, you have solved a problem and come up with an architecture-level solution. If you encounter a similar problem in any other application, the thought process (architecture or design) that was developed earlier should be reused. There is no point in revisiting the same problem and devising a solution, which is essentially reinventing the wheel.

The causes that lead to reinventing the wheel are as follows:

- An absence of a central documentation or repository that talks about architecture-level problems and solutions implemented
- A lack of communication between technology leaders in the community or company
- Building from scratch is the process followed in the organization; basically, immature processes and loose process implementation and adherence

The consequences of this AntiPattern include the following:

- Too many solutions to solve one standard problem, with many of them not being well thought out
- More time and resource utilization for the engineering team leading to overbudgeting and more time to market
- A closed system architecture (architecture useful for only one product), duplication of efforts, and poor risk management

Vendor lock-in

As the name of the AntiPattern suggests, product companies tend to be dependent on some of the technologies provided by their vendors. These technologies are so glued to their system that it is very difficult to move away.

The following are the causes of a vendor lock-in:

- Familiarity with folks in authority in the vendor company and possible discounts in the technology purchase
- Technology chosen based on the marketing and sales pitch instead of technology evaluation
- Using a proven technology (proven indicates that the return on investments with this technology were really high in the previous experience) in the current project even when it's not suited for project needs or requirements
- Technologists/developers are already trained in using this technology

The consequences of a vendor lock-in are as follows:

- Release cycles and product maintenance cycles of a company's product releases are directly dependent on the vendor's release time frame
- The product is developed around the technology rather than on the customer's requirements
- The product's time to market is unreliable and doesn't meet customer's expectations

Design by committee

Sometimes, based on the process in an organization, a group of people sit together and design a particular system. The resulting software architecture is often complex or substandard because it involves too many thought processes, and technologists who may not have the right skillset or experience in designing the products have put forward the ideas.

The causes of design by committee are as follows:

- The process in the organization involves getting the architecture or design approved by many stakeholders
- No single point of contact or architect responsible for the design
- The design priorities set by marketing or technologists rather than set by customer feedback

The symptoms observed with this AntiPattern include the following:

- Conflicting viewpoints between developers and architects even after the design is finalized
- Overly complex design that is very difficult to document
- Any change in the specification or design undergoes review by many, resulting in implementation delays

Summary

To summarize this chapter, you learned about AntiPatterns, what they are, and their classifications. We understood that AntiPatterns could be related to software development or software architecture. We looked at the commonly occurring AntiPatterns and learned about their causes, symptoms, and consequences. I am sure you will learn from these and avoid such situations in your project.

This is it folks, this was the last chapter of the book. Hope you enjoyed it and the book helped you improve your skills. Wish you all the very best!

Index

A

Abstract Factory pattern
  about 26, 32, 33
  implementing 34-36
  versus Factory method pattern 36
abstraction
  about 5
  features 5
Adapter pattern 40
AntiPattern
  benefits 128
  categories 129
  causes 132
  consequences 133
  defining 128
  results 128
aspects, object-oriented programming
  abstraction 5
  composition 6
  encapsulation 3
  inheritance 4
  polymorphism 4

B

bad design
  Fragile 128
  Immobile 128
  Rigid 128
  Viscose 128
Behavioral patterns
  properties 12
Bridge pattern 40

C

classes 2
client 43
Command design pattern
  defining 74-76
Command pattern
  advantages 83
  asynchronous task execution 82
  defining 74
  design considerations 79-82
  disadvantages 83
  implementing 79
  Redo or rollback operations 82
  UML class diagram 76-78
composition 6
Compound patterns 100
context, design patterns
  non-functional requirements 10
  participants 10
  results 10
  trade-offs 10
copy-and-paste or cut-and-paste
    programming
  causes 131
  consequences 132
  defining 131
core concepts, object-oriented programming
  classes 2
  methods 3
  objects 2
Creational patterns
  properties 11

D

Decorator pattern 40
design by committee
  causes 134
  symptoms 134
design patterns
  about 8
  advantages 10
  applicability 10
  Behavioral patterns 12
  classifying 11
  Creational patterns 11
  features 9
  Structural patterns 12
  taxonomy 10
dynamic languages
  patterns 11

E

encapsulation
  about 3
  features 3
examples, Structural design patterns
  Adapter pattern 40
  Bridge pattern 40
  Decorator pattern 40

F

façade 42
Façade design pattern
  about 40, 41
  and Proxy pattern, comparing 58
  implementing, in real world 43-47
factory
  advantages 26
Factory method pattern
  about 26-29
  advantages 32
  implementing 29-32
  versus Abstract Factory pattern 36
Factory pattern
  about 25
  Abstract Factory pattern 26, 32, 33

Factory method pattern 26-29
Simple Factory pattern 26-28

G

GoF (Gang of Four) 9
Golden Hammer
  causes 130
  consequences 130

H

handlers
  defining 108
  IndexHandler 108
  NewHandler 108
  UpdateHandler 108
Hollywood principle 97

I

inheritance 4
interface segregation principle
  about 7
  advantages 8
inversion of control principle
  about 7
  advantages 7

L

Lava Flow
  about 131
  causes 131
  symptoms 131
Loose coupling 70

M

metaclasses 18
methods 3
Model-View-Controller (MVC)
  about 99
  benefits 114
  Controller 103-105
  defining 100-102, 107
  design considerations 107
  Model 102

UML class diagram 105-107
View 103
working 100
module-level Singletons
defining 16
modules
defining 107-113
Monostate Singleton pattern
defining 16, 17
MTV (Model, Template, View) 107

O

object-oriented design principles
about 6
interface segregation principle 7
inversion of control principle 7
open/close principle 6
single responsibility principle 8
substitution principle 8
object-oriented programming
about 2
aspects 3
core concepts 3
Observer pattern
about 70
advantages 71
disadvantages 71
Observer pattern methods
pull model 69
push model 70
open/close principle
about 6
advantages 7

P

participants, State design pattern
ConcreteState 118
Context 118
State 118
polymorphism
about 4
features 4
principle of least knowledge 47
private keyword 4
protected keyword 4

Proxy design pattern
defining 50, 51
UML class diagram 52, 53
Proxy pattern
advantages 58
and Façade pattern, comparing 58
defining 54-57
using 50
Proxy types
defining 53
protective proxy 54
remote proxy 53
smart proxy 54
virtual proxy 53
public keyword 4
pull model 69
push model 70
Python 11

S

Simple Factory pattern 26-28
single responsibility principle
about 8
advantages 8
Singleton design pattern
classical singleton, implementing
in Python 14, 15
drawbacks 23
lazy instantiation 15
part 1, defining 19-21
part 2, defining 21-23
Singletons 18, 23
software architecture AntiPatterns
about 132
design by committee 133
vendor lock-in 133
wheel, reinventing 132
software development AntiPatterns
copy-and-paste or cut-and-paste
programming 131
defining 129
Golden Hammer 130
Lava Flow 131
spaghetti code 129
Software Development Life Cycle (SDLC) 9

Spaghetti code
causes 129
State design pattern
advantages 125
defining 117, 118
defining, with UML diagram 120
disadvantages 125
example 120, 121
with v3.5 implementation 122-124
working 118, 119
stock trading system
implementing 80, 81
Structural design patterns
about 40
examples 40
properties 12
substitution principle 8

T

taxonomy, design patterns
design 10
pattern 10
snippet 10
standard 10
Template Method 86

Template Method design pattern
about 92-97
advantages 97
defining 86-90, 95
design considerations 92, 93
disadvantages 97
hook, defining 96
UML class diagram 90-92
using 86
Tornado web application framework
URL 107

U

UML class diagram
about 41
client 42, 43
façade 42
system 42

V

vendor lock-in
causes 133
consequences 133

Thank you for buying
Learning Python Design Patterns
Second Edition

About Packt Publishing

Packt, pronounced 'packed', published its first book, *Mastering phpMyAdmin for Effective MySQL Management*, in April 2004, and subsequently continued to specialize in publishing highly focused books on specific technologies and solutions.

Our books and publications share the experiences of your fellow IT professionals in adapting and customizing today's systems, applications, and frameworks. Our solution-based books give you the knowledge and power to customize the software and technologies you're using to get the job done. Packt books are more specific and less general than the IT books you have seen in the past. Our unique business model allows us to bring you more focused information, giving you more of what you need to know, and less of what you don't.

Packt is a modern yet unique publishing company that focuses on producing quality, cutting-edge books for communities of developers, administrators, and newbies alike. For more information, please visit our website at www.packtpub.com.

About Packt Open Source

In 2010, Packt launched two new brands, Packt Open Source and Packt Enterprise, in order to continue its focus on specialization. This book is part of the Packt Open Source brand, home to books published on software built around open source licenses, and offering information to anybody from advanced developers to budding web designers. The Open Source brand also runs Packt's Open Source Royalty Scheme, by which Packt gives a royalty to each open source project about whose software a book is sold.

Writing for Packt

We welcome all inquiries from people who are interested in authoring. Book proposals should be sent to author@packtpub.com. If your book idea is still at an early stage and you would like to discuss it first before writing a formal book proposal, then please contact us; one of our commissioning editors will get in touch with you.

We're not just looking for published authors; if you have strong technical skills but no writing experience, our experienced editors can help you develop a writing career, or simply get some additional reward for your expertise.

Learning Python Design Patterns

ISBN: 978-1-78328-337-8   Paperback: 100 pages

A practical and fast-paced guide exploring python design patterns

1. Explore the Model-View-Controller pattern and learn how to build a URL shortening service.

2. All design patterns use a real-world example that can be modified and applied in your software.

3. No unnecessary theory! The book consists of only the fundamental knowledge that you need to know.

Expert Python Programming

ISBN: 978-1-84719-494-7   Paperback: 372 pages

Best practices for designing, coding, and distributing your Python software

1. Learn Python development best practices from an expert, with detailed coverage of naming and coding conventions.

2. Apply object-oriented principles, design patterns, and advanced syntax tricks.

3. Manage your code with distributed version control.

Please check **www.PacktPub.com** for information on our titles

Building Machine Learning Systems with Python

ISBN: 978-1-78216-140-0   Paperback: 290 pages

Master the art of machine learning with Python and build effective machine learning systems with this intensive hands-on guide

1. Master Machine Learning using a broad set of Python libraries and start building your own Python-based ML systems.

2. Covers classification, regression, feature engineering, and much more guided by practical examples.

Learning Python Data Visualization

ISBN: 978-1-78355-333-4   Paperback: 212 pages

Master how to build dynamic HTML5-ready SVG charts using Python and the pygal library

1. A practical guide that helps you break into the world of data visualization with Python.

2. Understand the fundamentals of building charts in Python.

3. Packed with easy-to-understand tutorials for developers who are new to Python or charting in Python.

Please check **www.PacktPub.com** for information on our titles

55686189R00092

Made in the USA
Lexington, KY
30 September 2016